JOYFUL INFOGRAPHICS

A friendly, human approach to data

Nigel Holmes

CRC Press
Taylor & Francis Group
Boca Raton London New York

CRC Press is an imprint of the
Taylor & Francis Group, an **informa** business

AN A K PETERS BOOK

AK Peters Visualization Series

This book is part of the AK Peters Visualization series, which aims to capture what visualization is today in all its variety and diversity, giving voice to researchers, practitioners, designers, and enthusiasts. Visualization plays an ever-more prominent role in the world, as we communicate about and analyze data. The series encompasses books from all subfields of visualization, including visual analytics, information visualization, scientific visualization, data journalism, infographics, and their connection to adjacent areas such as text analysis, digital humanities, data art, or augmented and virtual reality.

Series Editors

Alberto Cairo, *University of Miami, USA*
Tamara Munzner, *University of British Columbia, Vancouver, Canada*

Recent titles

Building Science Graphics
An Illustrated Guide to Communicating Science through Diagrams and Visualizations
Jen Christiansen

Joyful Infographics
A Friendly, Human Approach to Data
Nigel Holmes

Questions in Dataviz
A Design-Driven Process for Data Visualization
Neil Richards

Making with Data
Physical Design and Craft in a Data-Driven World
Edited by Samuel Huron, Till Nagel, Lora Oehlberg, Wesley Willett

Mobile Data Visualization
Edited by Bongshin Lee, Raimund Dachselt, Petra Isenberg, Eun Kyoung Choe

Data Sketches
Nadieh Bremer, Shirley Wu

Visualizing with Text
Richard Brath

Interactive Visual Data Analysis
Christian Tominski, Heidrun Schumann

Data-Driven Storytelling
Nathalie Henry Riche, Christophe Hurter, Nicholas Diakopoulos, Sheelagh Carpendale

For more information about this series please visit:
https://www.routledge.com/AK-Peters-Visualization-Series/book-series/CRCVIS

Foreword

The main goal of a visualization is to reveal and inform, but what if it could also make us smile? Humor—particularly the type of genial humor that Nigel Holmes has always favored in his long and fruitful career—can be a powerful tool in capable hands. This book, which we think is a great peek into the way Nigel thinks about design, explains why, when, and how to use such a tool.

Not so long ago, humor in visualization had bad press. Some popular authors extolled the alleged virtues of spare visual styles, rejected any joy not derived from the ecstatic contemplation of data, and chastised designers who inserted ornament into their visualizations. Such authors were sometimes understood—or, better said, *misunderstood*— as outlining universal rules of visualization, when in reality they were simply making a persuasive case for their own design preferences and for their personal opinions about elegance, truth, and goodness.

Nigel Holmes makes his own persuasive case in *Joyful Infographics*: humorous elements, if they don't distort the information represented in the graphic, aren't just decoration; they are harmless, and in certain cases they can even be beneficial, as recent research tentatively suggests: a touch of humor in a visualization—if it's sensible and appropriate, depending on factors such as topic or audience—may make it warmer, friendlier, more approachable, and inviting. Perhaps it's time to smile a bit more.

Alberto Cairo, *University of Miami, USA*
Tamara Munzner, *University of British Columbia, Vancouver, Canada*

Some images have been greatly reduced
from their original published size in magazines or books.

This symbol ⊕ next to an image means that
they are on the book's website
joyfulinfographics.com
where you can enlarge them
and give your tired eyes
a break.

First edition published 2023
by CRC Press
6000 Broken Sound Parkway NW, Suite 300, Boca Raton, FL 33487-2742

and by CRC Press
4 Park Square, Milton Park, Abingdon, Oxon, OX14 4RN

Library of Congress Cataloging-in-Publication Data
Names: Holmes, Nigel, 1942- author.
Title: Joyful infographics: a friendly, human approach to data / Nigel Holmes.

Description: First edition. | Boca Raton: AK Peters, CRC Press, 2023. |
Series: AK Peters visualization series | Includes bibliographical references and index.
Identifiers: LCCN 2022022725 (print) | LCCN 2022022726 (ebook) | ISBN
9781032119656 (hbk) | ISBN 9781032115580 (pbk) | ISBN 9781003222361 (ebk)
Subjects: LCSH: Information visualization. | Graphic arts. | Caricatures and cartoons.

Classification: LCC QA76.9.I52 H656 2023 (print) | LCC QA76.9.I52 (ebook)
| DDC 001.4/226--dc23/eng/20220527
LC record available at https://lccn.loc.gov/2022022725
LC ebook record available at https://lccn.loc.gov/2022022726

ISBN: 9781032119656 (hbk)
ISBN: 9781032115580 (pbk)
ISBN: 9781003222361 (ebk)

DOI: 10.1201/9781003222361

Publisher's note: This book has been prepared from camera-ready copy provided by the author.

Contents

Dedication

To Nannie Hay,
who lived with us and taught me to read
while my father fought in North Africa and Italy,
and my mother drove ambulances in Hull,
Yorkshire, during World War 2.

Nannie

*My brother,
Jeremy*

Me

*Off to the seaside
with bucket and spade.*

Warming up

Let's begin with some stretches.

I was a late comer to exercising regularly (three times a week, if I try hard). I don't love it, but it's important. We sit at our computers most of the time. It's good to give the body a break and move around. At least we should stretch our fingers.

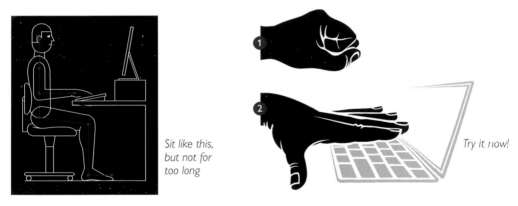

Sit like this, but not for too long

Try it now!

Wait, you thought this was a book about infographics?

Stretching is like sketching; you are getting ready for the real work(out) to follow. I made visual notes when I started to work with a trainer in 2007, because I needed reminders about his exercises on the days I wasn't working out with him. After a rotator cuff shoulder injury a few years later, I made more finished memory aids, for myself and the sports therapist *(below).*

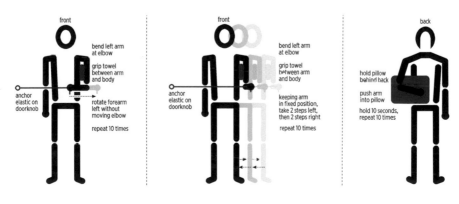

My trainer's routines were fleshed out in various magazine commissions, and I included one in a spread from my book *Instant Expert*. I've used part of that graphic to draw attention to some of ideas in the book you are reading now *(opposite)*.

When I exercise (at a local YMCA) I find a room where there's no loud music. I suppose the people who run the gym assume that energetic rock and rap helps you to be energetic, pumping you up. For me silence is better. It's the same with infographics: leaving space—white space, where data can breathe—is important. Exercising in silence also gives you space and time to think about what you should be getting on with: for about a year, that's been writing this book. Ever ready with a pencil and paper, I interrupt grunting on the floor to scribble quick thoughts that I might forget back at the computer. Ideas come at the oddest times. Take notes.

Try a few of these stretches at home. No gym necessary. *(Below, classic yoga sun salutation.)*

Exercise graphics for two magazines: Sports Illustrated for Women...   ...and Details

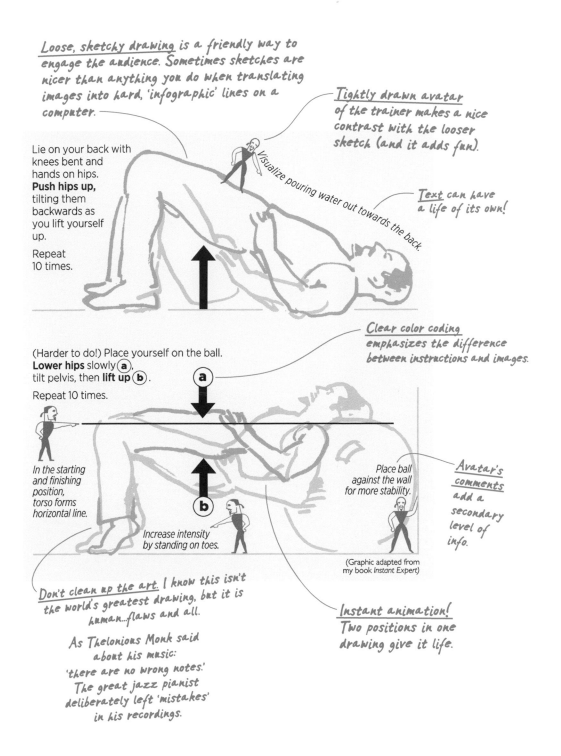

Loose, sketchy drawing is a friendly way to engage the audience. Sometimes sketches are nicer than anything you do when translating images into hard, 'infographic' lines on a computer.

Tightly drawn avatar of the trainer makes a nice contrast with the looser sketch (and it adds fun).

Lie on your back with knees bent and hands on hips. **Push hips up,** tilting them backwards as you lift yourself up.

Repeat 10 times.

Visualize pouring water out towards the back.

Text can have a life of its own!

Clear color coding emphasizes the difference between instructions and images.

(Harder to do!) Place yourself on the ball. **Lower hips** slowly (a), tilt pelvis, then **lift up** (b).

Repeat 10 times.

In the starting and finishing position, torso forms horizontal line.

Increase intensity by standing on toes.

Place ball against the wall for more stability.

Avatar's comments add a secondary level of info.

(Graphic adapted from my book Instant Expert)

Don't clean up the art. I know this isn't the world's greatest drawing, but it is human...flaws and all.

As Thelonious Monk said about his music: 'there are no wrong notes.' The great jazz pianist deliberately left 'mistakes' in his recordings.

Instant animation! Two positions in one drawing give it life.

Feeling better (or at least virtuous)? Now, on to the book itself...

Introduction

First, definitions of *Joyful* and *Infographics*.

I have long advocated using a touch of humor in information graphics as a way to make friends with readers, to help them relax when confronted with a string of numbers or obscure scientific concepts. My goal has always been to make reading, understanding, and looking at graphics, a pleasurable experience—not like homework. If I can raise a smile, I'll be half-way to helping readers see what I am trying to explain. That smile is a smile of recognition, a realization that what I'm doing is using a visual language—and an approach in general—that is friendly and understandable, however complex the data or difficult the subject matter. There's a whole school of thought that loathes this idea—it is precisely the lighter approach that upsets the guardians of humorless, minimalist, statistical purity. Apparently, any deviation from, or addition to 'just the facts' is wrong. Dreadfully wrong. Important-sounding pseudo-scientific theories such as *'optimal data-ink ratio'* are invoked. Architect Adolf Loos' 1910 lecture *Ornament and Crime* was a big influence on ivory-tower-dwelling chart purists, and Mies van de Rohe's famous *'less is more'* phrase became the overriding graphic tenet.

It's time to cue the equally famous *'less is a bore,'* from Robert Venturi, another architect. Why *do* architects have the best quotes?

When it comes to the role of humor in communication, I like this quote from the legendary graphic designer Paul Rand about avoiding visual gimmicks in annual reports. This is from his *Thoughts on Design* (1947):

'The visual message which professes to be profound or elegant often boomerangs as mere pretension; and the frame of mind which looks at humor as trivial and flighty mistakes the shadow for the substance. In short, the notion that the humorous approach to visual communication is undignified or belittling is sheer nonsense … "True humor," says Thomas Carlyle, "springs not more from the head than from the heart; it is not contempt, its essence is love, it issues not in laughter, but in still smiles, which lie far deeper."'

Well said, Paul and Tom (and I bet Dick and Harry agree).

'Humorous' might not be the right description of my approach. I am not suggesting that all infographics (or any of them, actually) should be funny. By humor, I mean good humor, a gentle friendliness, and joy and joyful capture that feeling. It's the delight in understanding—seeing—the story inside a dense data set or a touchy subject. I know that some things that we are called upon to explain need to be treated with extreme care. There's no room for fun in a graphic about cancer, or inequality, or terrorism, or abortion, but these subjects and many others nevertheless deserve a clear, reader-friendly treatment. A load of data, dumped in front of readers, viewers or users may contain all the facts, but it doesn't necessarily explain them, and might even scare the intended audience away. *Joyful* in this sense, means happily revealing the meaning.

Infographics are easier to define. They are simply what the word itself says: information, presented graphically. Infographics have a visual component—sometimes it's a pictorial representation of the subject, sometimes abstract bars and lines—and there's usually some explanatory text, too. I'm including maps, charts, diagrams, instructions, signs, and symbols in the definition.

I should note that the word 'graphic' is also used to describe a vividly detailed description or visualization, which might even come with a warning that it could offend or shock. But a shock of recognition is just a small step beyond the smile of recognition that I'm seeking, and while I don't intend to shock, I find clarity, paired with a friendly approach even when dealing with shocking information, is a good way to explain it.

Most of my work has been for print—magazines and newspapers—lots of it before 'infographics' was a word. In their book *Eyes on the News,* Mario Garcia and Pegie Stark studied how readers generally approach the printed page: first, they are drawn to the pictures or graphics, especially if they are colored, then they read the captions and headline and perhaps the first few lines of text, and only then do they commit to reading the whole article. Clearly, pictures, infographics, maps, and icons are powerful attractants.

When first I arrived at *Time* magazine in 1977, some writers, especially those working in the *Economy and Business* section, balked at my graphics being prominently displayed at the top of their pages. What's more, the graphics were bigger than they had been under previous editors, so the writers were upset at losing precious space for their words. It was only when the magazine got letters from readers telling us that they could understand the stories better now that there was some graphic help on the page, that the formerly disgruntled writers willingly gave up some of the proverbial 1,000 words for a picture. (Or 10,000 words if you think that famous maxim should be attributed to Confucius. Newspaper editor Arthur Brisbane, in an article about journalism and publicity in 1911, seems to have been the source that reduced the number to 1,000.) I don't think a picture, or a graphic, is worth a thousand words; it's worth exactly as many words as are needed to explain what it's replacing.

My hope is that *Joyful Infographics* will show you some ways to help readers understand more clearly what you are explaining to them, and at the same time make them feel good about that understanding. And I hope it will help you make your 'pictures' worthy of those 1,000—or 10,000—words.

That graphic had better be worth it!

writer

1,000

10,000

Don't be afraid of white space.

Well, get these friggin' speech balloons out of here, then!

2

Influences

There was one artist in my family, dad's uncle George. At Christmas, his cards were hand-printed etchings of country scenes. He was an engineer, working in his father's tannery, but he had a particular interest in sailing, and he drew the local commercial fishing sailboats that worked in the North Sea and along England's coasts. The drawings were immaculate engineers' plans and side views of boats, very different from the sketchiness of his Christmas etchings.

Great Uncle George…

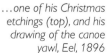
…one of his Christmas etchings (top), and his drawing of the canoe yawl, Eel, 1896

What fascinated me more than the etchings was his black and white map of the River Hull that hung in our living room. It was a straightforward, flat map of the river (a tributary of the much larger River Humber) that flowed through the center of the City of Hull, in Yorkshire, about 10 miles east of the village of Swanland, where we lived. Arranged around the map, *(opposite)* George had drawn realistic bridges that spanned the river, appearing as you would see them if you were walking there. I loved the combination of two- and three-dimensional graphics in one picture.

Years later, I was commissioned by the *Observer* magazine to draw the fishing fleet that used to sail around England's coasts. The magazine's art director, Brian Haynes, gave me a set of old plans of these boats to use as reference. They were great uncle George's drawings.

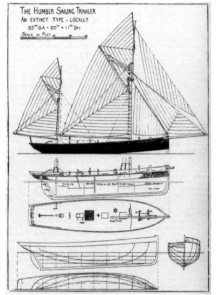

One of the drawings that Brian gave me as reference…

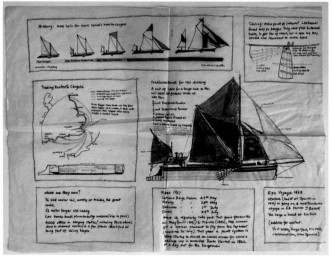

…and the first sketch I made for the job

Next pages: some of my drawings from the Observer article.

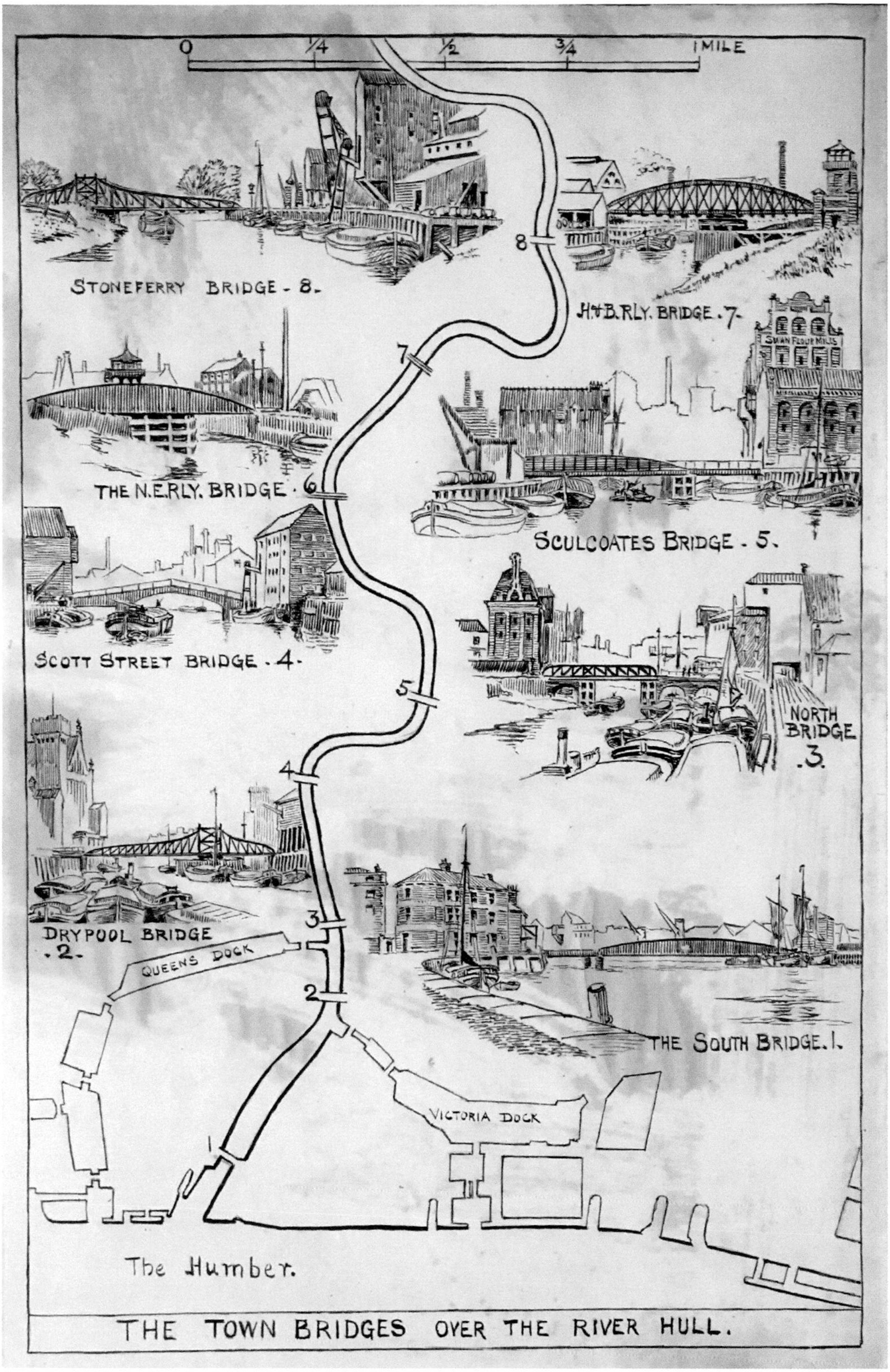

THE TOWN BRIDGES OVER THE RIVER HULL.

Norfolk Wherry

Humber Keel Boat

Aldeburgh Sprat Boat

Galway Hooker

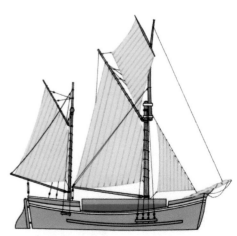

Severn Trow

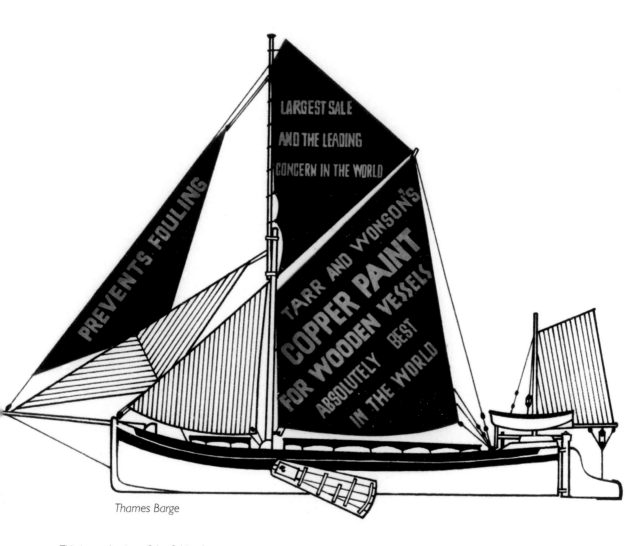

Thames Barge

This is a selection of the fishing boats
I drew in 1969 for the Observer
Magazine, based on great uncle
George's drawings.

It would have been an easier job if I'd
had a computer then!

The ones on the left are all drawn to
the same scale; this page is enlarged.

About the same time that I was engrossed by George's river map, aged nine or ten, I 'borrowed' an atlas from my older brother, Jeremy, and never gave it back. *A Pictorial Atlas of the British Isles,* by H. Alnwick, published in 1937, was filled with tiny, colorful illustrations of people swarming all over the land masses. Bordering each spread were black silhouettes of men, women, and children working and playing, together with buildings, factories, trains, and bridges. There was a gentle sense of humor about the whole book—I imagined conversations going on between the little people standing up on the maps—it showed me that geography could be fun. Just like the drawings on uncle George's map, the little figures added a human touch, but were also informative. I used the book as a real reference atlas for a little too long!

From the 'borrowed' atlas: we lived in Swanland, a little village about 6 miles east of Hull (number 35, above)

In England there's a love of silliness, and many of the influences on my work have little to do with information design, but are important to fostering my sense of humor. Most nights, after a family dinner, my dad would suddenly get up and leave the room, only to return a minute later wearing an old hat of his (or one of my mother's) pulled down to his eyebrows. It made us all laugh. No sooner had he done this little performance, he left the room just as abruptly, and then would reappear, innocently oblivious, as though nothing had happened.

We were probably eating chocolates during these antics. Unlike Forrest Gump's maxim from his mama, *'Life is like a box of chocolates. You never know what you're gonna get,'* we knew exactly what we were gonna get, because there was a little graphic with a picture of each one right there in the box. (Listen to the George Harrison song *Savoy Truffle* on the Beatles' *White*

Album; it's an almost literal recitation of the list inside Mackintosh's Good News chocolates. Not counting uncle George's map, those explanatory diagrams were my first encounter with joyful infographics. I liked the chocolates, too.

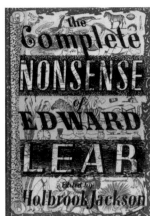

A map of the Beatles' inspiration   *Cover by Barnett Freedman*

My father gave me a book of Edward Lear's nonsense poems (*The Owl and the Pussycat, etc.*) and limericks (*'There was an old lady from…'*). It had a wonderful cover by Barnett Freedman. Lear's scratchy illustrations were just right for the silliness of his poems. They were nothing like his watercolors of exotic landscapes in far-off lands, or his paintings of parrots, drawn life-size from live and stuffed examples, for the Zoological Society in 1830–32, when he was 20.

Talking of parrots, John Cleese's sketch about trying to return a dead one to the pet store that sold it to him, from *Monty Python's Flying Circus,* which started on BBC TV in 1969, still makes me laugh. The whole *Monty Python* troupe lampooned English attitudes and class divisions. They made fun of pomposity, urging us not to take anything, especially ourselves, too seriously.

John Cleese from the Ministry of Silly Walks

Python was following in the footsteps of a classic BBC radio program from the 1950s, *The Goon Show,* which starred comedian Michael Bentine, Harry Secombe (a great Welsh singer), Spike Milligan (a manically funny guy), and an as yet unfamous Peter Sellers. The four of them played with words, sounds and non sequiturs. When I was in hospital after having had my appendix removed, I was given headphones to listen to the radio, but I had to take them off because I couldn't stop laughing at the *Goons.* It hurt my stomach too much.

At boarding school, I was thrilled to get *Punch* magazine every week, forwarded on to me from a favorite aunt, rolled up in a special brown paper mailing thing. As well as the satirical articles and cartoons—my favorite *Punch* cartoonist, and some-time Art Editor, was Kenneth Bird, who signed his spare, single-line drawings 'Fougasse'—the magazine's advertisements often included tiny infographics in red and black *(a detail, below).*

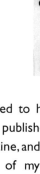

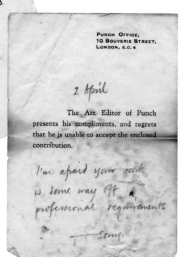

I longed to have a cartoon published in the magazine, and sent them some of my efforts. I can't find whatever it was that I sent but I did keep the rejection slips *(left)*. Some kind person in the office took the trouble to write a friendly note on them.

Two eccentric Englishmen, the photographer Eadweard Muybridge (with a splendidly odd first name), and the sculptor, letterer, and artist Eric Gill had a big impact on me. Muybridge was taking photos of the American West when he was hired in 1878 by Leland Stanford, the founder of Stanford University, to prove the theory (and potentially win a bet) that at some point during a horse's gallop, all four hooves are off the ground at the same time. Muybridge lined up 12 cameras in a row, with trip wires extending from their shutter mechanisms to a white board wall. A horse and jockey galloped across the front of the wall, tripping the wires as they swept past, thus taking a sequence of 12 separate still photographs of animal and rider in motion. Stanford's theory was proved. *(Opposite.)*

Apart from the beautiful simplicity of the images themselves, Muybridge's sequences of different animals and humans in motion are a great resource for artists to see how animals and people really move. Many graphic designers, myself included, have traced his photographs. I hope we have not forgotten how revolutionary they were.

My other eccentric English influencer, Eric Gill, created simple, black & white wood engravings, and also the typeface Gill Sans (1928-30), which he based on classical Roman engraved

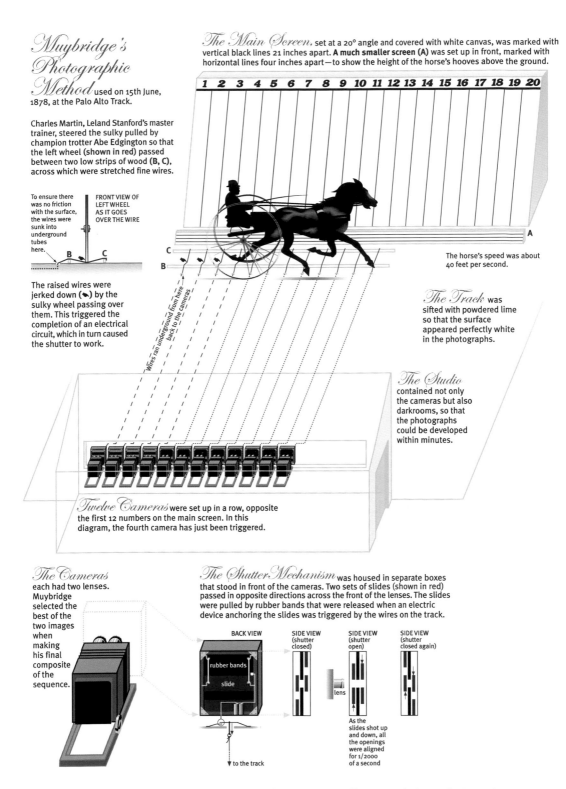

Muybridge's Photographic Method used on 15th June, 1878, at the Palo Alto Track.

Charles Martin, Leland Stanford's master trainer, steered the sulky pulled by champion trotter Abe Edgington so that the left wheel (shown in red) passed between two low strips of wood (B, C), across which were stretched fine wires.

To ensure there was no friction with the surface, the wires were sunk into underground tubes here.

FRONT VIEW OF LEFT WHEEL AS IT GOES OVER THE WIRE

B C

The raised wires were jerked down (↘) by the sulky wheel passing over them. This triggered the completion of an electrical circuit, which in turn caused the shutter to work.

The Main Screen, set at a 20° angle and covered with white canvas, was marked with vertical black lines 21 inches apart. A much smaller screen (A) was set up in front, marked with horizontal lines four inches apart—to show the height of the horse's hooves above the ground.

1 2 3 4 5 6 7 8 9 10 11 12 13 14 15 16 17 18 19 20

A

The horse's speed was about 40 feet per second.

C

B

Wires ran underground from here back to the cameras

The Track was sifted with powdered lime so that the surface appeared perfectly white in the photographs.

The Studio contained not only the cameras but also darkrooms, so that the photographs could be developed within minutes.

Twelve Cameras were set up in a row, opposite the first 12 numbers on the main screen. In this diagram, the fourth camera has just been triggered.

The Cameras each had two lenses. Muybridge selected the best of the two images when making his final composite of the sequence.

The Shutter Mechanism was housed in separate boxes that stood in front of the cameras. Two sets of slides (shown in red) passed in opposite directions across the front of the lenses. The slides were pulled by rubber bands that were released when an electric device anchoring the slides was triggered by the wires on the track.

BACK VIEW

rubber bands

slide

to the track

SIDE VIEW (shutter closed)

SIDE VIEW (shutter open)

SIDE VIEW (shutter closed again)

lens

As the slides shot up and down, all the openings were aligned for 1/2000 of a second

How Muybridge set up his cameras to prove that all four hooves are off the ground when galloping

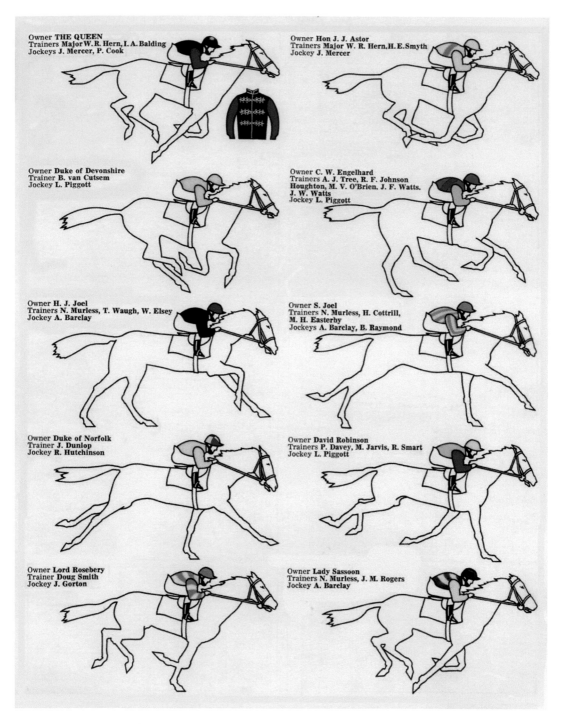

Owner THE QUEEN
Trainers Major W. R. Hern, I. A. Balding
Jockeys J. Mercer, P. Cook

Owner Hon J. J. Astor
Trainers Major W. R. Hern, H. E. Smyth
Jockey J. Mercer

Owner Duke of Devonshire
Trainer B. van Cutsem
Jockey L. Piggott

Owner C. W. Engelhard
Trainers A. J. Tree, R. F. Johnson
Houghton, M. V. O'Brien, J. F. Watts.
J. W. Watts
Jockey L. Piggott

Owner H. J. Joel
Trainers N. Murless, T. Waugh, W. Elsey
Jockey A. Barclay

Owner S. Joel
Trainers N. Murless, H. Cottrill,
M. H. Easterby
Jockeys A. Barclay, B. Raymond

Owner Duke of Norfolk
Trainer J. Dunlop
Jockey R. Hutchinson

Owner David Robinson
Trainers P. Davey, M. Jarvis, R. Smart
Jockey L. Piggott

Owner Lord Rosebery
Trainer Doug Smith
Jockey J. Gorton

Owner Lady Sassoon
Trainers N. Murless, J. M. Rogers
Jockey A. Barclay

*Shameless tracing: identifying different owners' colors, from Radio Times, June 1970.
Muybridge was a big help! (Top right shows all four hooves off the ground.)*

letterforms and proportions that gave his font the same easy legibility as a serif face, in contrast to the more mechanical sans fonts that were popular at the time. Gill was interested in giving people a pleasant, but still 'modern' reading experience. Gill Sans remains one of the only sans serif fonts that one might use for the entire text of a book, like this one.

Eric Gill wore an odd hat…   *…but drew a lovely font*

In 1966, I traveled around America in a Greyhound bus. An advertisement (or what remains of it, since I haphazardly cut it out of a magazine) for something to do with 'high-treated alloy steel' had a huge influence on me. Lines in your artwork didn't have to be black! You'd still draw them in black, but then instruct the printer to print them in a color. My eyes were opened to production possibilities: drawing could now be excitingly separated from the way it appeared in print. This was 11 years before Steve Jobs and Steve Wozniak introduced the Apple 1 in 1976, and a further 8 years before we had Macintoshes, by which time my small insight would be thought pathetically naïve.

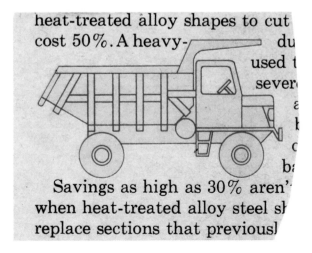

This simple thing opened the way to a kind of graphic freedom.

Music might seem to be an odd influence. I listen to jazz a lot, and accompany my favorite musicians on drums when no one is listening. Pianist Thelonious Monk's odd use of silence taught me the value of adding empty space to graphics, allowing important parts to be 'heard.' Also, Monk had huge hands, leading some to think that this accounted for 'mistakes' when he played. What sounded like slip-ups made Monk all the more human to me. Monk said: 'There are no wrong notes.'

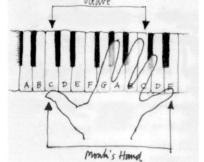

Monk's big hand

Miles' simplicity

in an article for the *Information Design Journal*, I wrote about how trumpeter Miles Davis influenced me: '*When designing an icon, I use the computer primarily to simplify the image; to find the most economical way to represent the subject; to take stuff away, rather than puffing it up by adding extraneous, and all-too-easily produced effects. Listening to Miles' early work—an unmistakable, simple sound—I see/hear the equivalent of a one-line drawing. He unfolded a spare line of melody, unfussy, and without the helter-skelter of notes that his fellow beboppers were playing at the time. In the same way, graphic symbols work best when they are simply conceived and executed. In both cases there is joy in recognizing elegant simplicity through economy of means.*'

John Adams is a modern classical composer, originally part of the minimalist school, but always with an undercurrent of humor. When his *Grand Pianola Music* was first played, many hated it. Adams says: '*The concept of entertaining your listener was verboten in the modernist period. Any entertainment had to be brutally ironic. Which Grand Pianola Music is not. Its humor is quintessentially American…*' He goes on: '*One of the dissatisfactions I had with modernism was its coldness. The expression of deep feelings was being co-opted by pop music. Music that touched you the way Beethoven or Bach did, or Wagner, Sibelius, Debussy—all that soul [in modernism] was being taken over by John Coltrane and the Beatles and Janis Joplin and Otis Redding.*'

Adams' quotes are included in Larry Rothe's liner notes from the *Grand Pianola Music* CD. That's where I discovered that Adams' later piece, *Absolute Jest*, also on the CD, was based on Beethoven's scherzos, or jokes. Beethoven included scherzos in his heavier stuff, to give his audience a break of sorts. Adams again: '*To Beethoven, a scherzo is this inspired sense of movement and happiness. I wanted my work to be invested with that happiness.*' Yesss.

The critic and author Kenneth Clark had similar opinions to Adams' about the rigidity of modernism—in Clark's case it was about abstract art. Here's what he said: '*Abstract art, in anything like a pure form, has the fatal defect of purity. Without a pinch of earth the artist soon contracts spiritual beriberi [a nasty disease] and dies of exhaustion.'* By 'pinch of earth' he meant a connection with landscape, atmosphere, and humanity. Some people considered Clark an old fuddy-duddy, but he tirelessly promoted contemporary English artists. And he thought about the audience for his books. His TV series *Civilization,* used straightforward, jargon-free language, so non-specialist readers and viewers could easily understand his points.

Another move away from long-held artistic 'rules' occurred around the idea that Greek and Roman sculptures were intended to be pure, undecorated white marble forms at the time they were made. When researchers discovered that some statues had been gaudily painted, and others naturalistically colored to make them look lifelike, purists insisted on clinging to the Renaissance-era myth that they had been totally white from the start. Examining microscopic scraps of paint in the sculpture's crevices, researchers proved the opposite was the case. But the idea that pure, cold, white sculpture should be defiled with bright color—oh, the horrors!

Less of a fuss was made about coloring the Temple of Dendur in the Metropolitan Museum of Art, New York, where it sits in serene beigeness. Instead of making replicas of the original, and then painting them—as was done with the Greek and Roman statues to show what they had originally looked like—the Met projected colors onto some of the actual low-relief images carved into the temple's walls, for a temporary exhibition in 2016–7. No one complained.

So…great uncle George's map; a children's atlas; English radio and television silliness; a satirical magazine; sequential photographs; a genial typeface; an American advertisement; space and simplicity in jazz; a revolt from the rules of musical and artistic modernism—I realize that some of my silly influences might not seem like good examples to follow when trying to explain things clearly. But just because a graphic is presented in a serious manner, does that automatically make it authoritative? And the opposite of that: just because a graphic is lighthearted, does that mean it's not authoritative? How many of us learn more about the serious news of the day from funny, satirical late-night TV news shows, than we do from network newscasts, or from newspapers, or from all-day pecking at our smart phones, rabbit-holing down the web? One of the best satirical TV hosts is John Oliver, who calls his work 'investigative comedy.' We laugh watching his show, but we remember the facts. We laugh, then we think.

As long as designers don't overload infographics with so much extraneous stuff that the meaning of the story is obscured, we shouldn't be afraid to add a feeling of approachability and humanity—even humor where appropriate—to our graphic toolboxes. Helping our audiences to understand the meaning of information is the point, isn't it? Rules be damned.

The next chapter is my selected history of infographics. Every one of the landmarks, from cave painting to Isotype has influenced me. How could they not? History is the great teacher.

Pictorial data through the ages

This is a personal timeline of influential infographic landmarks. Information designers use elements of this list every day, whether consciously or not, and whole books have been written about each of them; my comments here scratch the surface, but it's sadly unsurprising that no woman appears until Emma Willard in 1835. (It's even sadder that we assume it was only men who painted in caves.) As with most other artistic and scientific work, history is not herstory. But read on—we make up for the omission in the 21st century.

45,000 to 16,000 years ago It all starts here.

I know it's a cliché to say that **cave painters** were the first infographic artists, but I'll say it again. We shouldn't be afraid of using clichés, even though a standard dictionary definition is 'a trite phrase, and the idea expressed by it; something that has become overly familiar or commonplace.' In my dictionary, the definition of cliché is 'obvious truth.'

I digress. What were the cave artists doing 40,000 years ago? They were showing, counting, listing, teaching, storytelling. That's a good description of infographics. Others have suggested that cave paintings were a sort of proto-cinema—helped by the flickering light of hand-held torches which seemed to animate the art—or that they were the first PowerPoint shows.

We speculate about why those painters drew and painted (and scratched) on the walls of their caves. Was there a spiritual connection? Art for art's sake? A pastime in cold winters? Target practice? (There are pock-marks on some of the images.) Animal identification? A way to honor animals seen and hunted? Why are many of the images painted on top of others?

Lots of questions. The *why* may be difficult, but there is no speculation about *what* they painted. It's all there in front of you. The earliest figurative art found so far—in 2017, but only published in 2021—is in the Leang Tedongnge Cave, on the island of Sulawesi. It's a picture of a warty pig (*right*), dated to be about 45,500 years old. Other recent discoveries in Indonesia include a picture of a wild bull dated at 44,000 years old, found in a cave in Borneo. In the Cave of  Maltravieso, in Spain, 'stenciled' handprints have been dated to 66,700 years ago. Like many such handprints found in old caves, these are more 'I was here' than art. Much older abstract markings have been found, notably in the Blombos Cave near Capetown, South Africa. These date from 75,000 to 100,000 years old. I'm interested in representational art; things that could be recognized as life outside the cave.

The paintings and drawings in the Chauvet and Lascaux caves were sometimes fully rendered and colored images, but just as often they were simple, flat silhouettes of horses, bison, big cats, (and a few humans). The artists drew only the essential details of their subjects, and that's what today's infographic illustrators do too, many thousands of years later. The reason for this, both then and now, is simple: showing the essential details of anything will convey your idea most efficiently. Cave art was not art for art's sake—for aesthetic appeal—it was the first graphic messaging. It wasn't interior decoration. After all, why paint on top of an existing image, spoiling it, instead of finding another stretch of blank wall or ceiling? Repetition was the painters' way to underline the original message on the wall—to emphasize it, to teach it again. And again, and again, and again to some 20,000 years of 'students,' 800 generations.

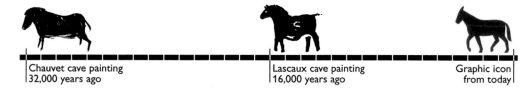

Chauvet cave painting
32,000 years ago

Lascaux cave painting
16,000 years ago

Graphic icon
from today

No one knows the mindset of these early artists, but I'd love to have a chat with them, if only to let them know how influential their work is today. It's humbling to look back and see that the simple, silhouetted animal drawings by early humans are strikingly similar to today's graphic icons of horses or on signs showing us where to see bison and big cats at the zoo.

5,000 years ago Line 'em up

Egyptian wall paintings were often designed to create a pleasant life after death, and were studied millenniums later by Neurath (see below, and later), who used the convention of lining up figures in a neat, countable formation in his work. Today, the same stylized view of people with heads in profile and bodies straight on—you know: 'Walk like an Egyptian'—is used for pedestrian crossing signs because this physically awkward arrangement of body parts actually shows the most instantly recognizable figure of a walking person. *(See traffic light signage.)*

c. 150 Map man

Ptolemy's Geographia laid down the basic rules of mapmaking. Despite a big mistake (oops, the Earth is the center of the universe), this work was the cartographic standard for the next 1,000 years. Ptolemy advanced the idea that maps could include climate, population density and birth rates. He saw maps as vehicles for information beyond literal geography.

In *Pictorial Maps,* I included a line about Mrs Ptolemy making a mean Greek salad, but my editor didn't think it was funny. Today, funny wouldn't come into it, I'd be censored for being sexist.

1066 Narrative art

The **Bayeaux Tapestry** (by the way, it's an embroidery not a tapestry) tells the story of the Norman conquest of England in a continuous band of sequential pictures. Is this the first comic strip? It's certainly a big one: 225ft (69m) long, and a bit under 2ft (0.6m) wide—a complete story in words and pictures.

The year 1066 is seared into the minds of many English schoolchildren as a result of reading *1066 And All That (A Memorable History of England, comprising all the parts you can remember, including 103 Good Things, 5 Bad Kings and 2 Genuine Dates)* when we were supposed to be studying proper history textbooks. It's a hilarious satire first published in 1930 by W.C. Sellar and R.J. Yeatman. When history reaches the Crimean War, Florence Nightingale is referred to as *Florence Nightingown, Flora MacNightshade,* and Flora *MacNightlight (the Lady with the Deadly Lampshade).* Like good satire, the facts are all there, embedded in the fun.

1480s Renaissance genius

Leonardo da Vinci drew things for himself in order to properly understand them. He made beautiful drawings and paintings, of course, but also charts, diagrams, pictorial maps, and anatomical cutaways—some of which he imagined, rather than directly observing them. He's the consummate infographics artist.

When I was 13, a beloved aunt (not Larry David's beloved 'aunt,' in the funniest episode of *Curb Your Enthusiasm!*) gave me a book of Leonardo's *Drawings*, and two volumes of his *Notebooks*. At the time, I gazed at the drawings, and ignored the texty notebooks. Later, when I was preparing a lecture that included a section about an enormous (modern) statue of a horse based on Leonardo's drawings, I looked up his notes on how to transfer the measurements of a life-sized clay sculpture of a horse to a block of marble for carving the finished piece, and also how much the final sculpture would cost, in ducats.

But I was immediately distracted by all sorts of other stuff: a cure for seasickness (the sap of wormwood); that a dead man will float in water on his back, while a dead woman will float face down; how to save yourself in the sea after a shipwreck (wear a coat made out of two layers of leather that are 'quite airtight.' Blow into the coat to inflate it and you'll float); and one piece of advice that I use all the time: '[study] as soon as you are awake or before you go to sleep in bed in the dark.' The 'dark' is his important point here, it allows your imagination to see what you have been working on in the light.

1658 Picturing the world

Orbis Sensualium Pictus,

A World of Things Obvious to the Senses, drawn in Pictures.

The Czech Jan Amos Comenius' textbook of visual aids for children, *Orbis Sensualium Pictus (The Visible World in Pictures),* was the first pictorial encyclopedia, and was printed in German and other European languages, not just Latin, like most educational books of the time. One part of it taught children the alphabet by mimicking animal sounds. Critics thought the realism of the pictures sometimes defeated its purpose. Hmmm, I've heard criticism like that before.

1630s Axis guy

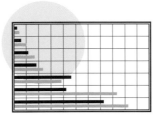

René Descartes' analytic geometry showed that two numbers could describe the position of a point on a surface by using two lines (the x axis and y axis, or coordinates) with scales and numbers on them. This is the Cartesian grid, the basis of the way we plot charts and graphs today. To this day, I have to think twice about which is the Y and which the X; I wish they were V and H, for Vertical and Horizontal. I'll try to remember that X is a cross (across).

1780s The first chartmaker

William Playfair invented the bar chart (1786), the line graph (1786), and the pie chart (1805). He insisted that his charts were pictures of numbers, not the numbers themselves. Instead of looking at a table of numbers, people would more easily remember them if they were presented as visual shapes—lines, bars, and pies. If they wanted the actual numbers, readers could consult the data he used to make the charts. In his **1786** book, *The Commercial and Political Atlas,* Playfair on bar charts: *'Suppose the money received by a man in trade were all in guineas, and that every evening he made a single pile of all the guineas received during the day, each pile would represent a day, and its height would be proportioned to the receipts of that day; so that by this plain operation, time, proportion, and amount, would all be physically combined.'*

The guinea was a silver coin in circulation at the time, and was worth about $4.20. After 1814, the last year the coin was minted, 'guinea' referred to a sum of one pound and one shilling, or about $1.40 today. (The word lives on: The 1,000 and 2,000 Guineas are names of horse races in England and Ireland.) Playfair systematized commercial data in order to help his readers understand it. He transformed numbers into 'pictures.'

1835 History in perspective

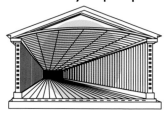

The educational reformer **Emma Willard** made *chronographers* (her name for illustrated timelines of history) often using perspective to show the passage of time—the further away from the front of the graphic, the older the date. In her *Picture of Nations, or Perspective Sketch of the Course of Empire* (1835), a neat little box of type explained that *'events apparently diminish when viewed through the vista of departed years…applying the principle to a practical purpose we have here brought before the eye, at once glance a sketch of the whole complicated subject of Universal History.'*

Perspective gave Willard a way to present recent events and dates larger and in more detail in the foreground of her graphics. Her amazingly intricate *chronographers* invited the reader to compare dates, (indeed whole periods of history), religions, rulers, and wars in one country to others that were geographically distant.

1858 Graphic trailblazer

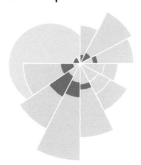

In 1858, **Florence Nightingale**—the 'Lady with the Lamp'—made a chart that some called a rose diagram, or polar area chart (although she preferred to call the slices of her chart 'wedges') to show seasonal causes of death before and after improved sanitation at the Barrack Hospital in Scutari, Istanbul, during the Crimean War, where she had volunteered to serve.

Nightingale was the founder of modern nursing. Her famous graphic persuaded British medical and military bigwigs to take notice of the lack of sanitation at the Scutari hospital. She could just as well have made a conventional bar chart from the data, but her unusual chart form made people see the problems. Her efforts eventually led to government passage of public health measures.

1920s Isotype

Austrian social scientist **Otto Neurath** and **Marie Reidemeister** (later Otto's wife) together with **Gerd Arntz** and other artists, collaborated on what has become a standard method of showing data pictorially. Neurath called his method *Isotype (International System of Typographic Picture Education)*. He insisted on 'statistical accountability' meaning that his team's work wasn't just an illustration with abstract bars attached to it; instead, the bars themselves in Isotype charts consisted of icons lined up in rows that represented the quantity of a commodity that could be counted—they were tiny pictures of whatever commodity was being charted—so you instantly knew what the graphic was about. Although Neurath famously said 'words divide, pictures unite, he did not think that Isotype constituted a complete visual language that could communicate everything by itself. Instead, he called his method a 'helping' language, one that perfectly married just the right amount of words with Arntz's beautifully drawn icons. Marie Neurath (1898-1986), continued her husband's infographic work after his death in 1945, primarily making informational books for children.

Otto and the surprisingly large number of others using his unit chart system (notably Rudolf Modley, who had worked with Neurath in Austria in the 1930s) are enjoying well-deserved, if somewhat late, recognition for their importance in making infographics accessible and understandable by all—the definition of joyful infographics! If I had to name one graphic hero, it would be Neurath (with Arntz a close second).

Red beard →

The young Otto Neurath …

… Marie Reidemeister …

… and Gerd Arntz

1926 Mechanical Anatomy

Working at the same time as Neurath, the German gynecologist **Fritz Kahn** art directed graphics that explained the workings of the human body as though they were machines. His most famous diagram, drawn by Fritz Schüler, was *Man as an Industrial Palace,* and it's just that: an almost life-sized cutaway of the human body, filled with pictorial metaphors for its basic systems: digestion, blood and air circulation, and nerves.

The work of these two pioneers, Neurath and Kahn—who apparently never met, and who both had to flee the Nazis—crossed language barriers in an effort to educate people in an approachable way. In 1943, Neurath said: *'One of our first principles was to make even the smallest chart as good, as original, and as charming as possible.'*

1933 The map as diagram

Harry Beck's diagram of the London Underground is the father of almost every transit map in the world. An engineering draughtsman working for a division of the Underground system, Beck drew a map that used one scale to show the large distances covered by trains in the suburbs, and a different scale to show the much busier, smaller central area of the city. Although not strictly a pictorial infographic, I've included Harry's abstract diagram-map in this list of influential landmarks because it embodies the idea of joyful infographics: beautiful, clear communication designed in an approachable way.

The graphic directly addresses its intended audience, ignoring above-ground geography and concentrating on the subway rider's essential question: what's the next station? It is many designers' favorite information graphic and has stood the test of time, with newly constructed lines periodically added to Harry's original map of six.* It was ground-breaking. (Pun intended.)

---

* To coincide with the Queen of England's Platinum Jubilee, Transport for London (TfL) issued a new map in May 2022 that included the new Elizabeth Line. It was met with dismay by mapmakers. Cartographer Ken Field says: *'The network has become so crowded. It's questionable whether Beck would have employed the same design philosophy had he wrestled with the current layout and requirements. The map now needs a redesign from first principles.'*

1940s and 50s Two magazines, two infographic giants

Fortune and *Time* had infographic artists on staff, and they published ground-breaking maps and diagrams. **Richard Edes Harrison**'s *Look at the World, The Fortune Atlas for World Strategy* (1944) includes maps drawn from unorthodox points of view: His Europe viewed from the East, or Japan from Siberia did not show landmasses the way we were used to seeing them in conventional atlases. They made you look and think anew. Often they were how the enemy viewed the US and Western Europe during WW2. Among other cartographic conventions, Harrison jettisoned the notion that North had to be at the top of the map.

Time's principal mapmaker, **Robert M. Chapin Jr**, did more straightforward cartography, but he wasn't shy about integrating pictorial elements to his maps—such as a realistically-drawn fist punching forward to show advancing troop movements. But his illustration never got in the way of accuracy. Indeed, his maps were used by the US government during the war.

When I arrived at *Time*, 35 years later, I found the archives of every map and chart that had appeared in the magazine since the 1920s. Chapin's maps with their bold metaphors gave me a kind of license to go back to more illustrative graphics than the straightforward approach the magazine had adopted during the 1950s. In this I was mentored and championed by the person who hired me to work at *Time*, the Art Director Walter Bernard, who had just redesigned it. Just for fun, I made myself a laminated, official-looking Artistic License, which allowed me, well, artistic license.

1990s to now Big data

At the end of the 20th century, I watched infographics veer from over-produced 3-d renderings, made possible by new computer programs, to cold, stripped-down minimalism.   As our machines got faster and more sophisticated, we started to call some of what we did Data Visualization. Infographics *are* data visualization, of course—both fields make data visible— but the computer-driven 'dataviz' world is different from the originally analog, more pictorial world of infographics. In sum, data visualizations *present* data. Infographics *explain* data. That's a big difference.

It sounds as though I'm dismissing data visualization in favor of an approach to making information understandable by making it more pictorial. Here's where I gladly acknowledge the attribute of data visualization that's not attainable in print: interactivity, on the web. I'm no expert on this—being principally a designer for print—but I know that the ability to handle large datasets, with instantly clickable details, represents a leap forward for the field. Interactivity can present a complex story, and let people decide for themselves which parts they want to explore. *Readers* are freed from static print when they become *users* on the web; they can manipulate and customize the data to see themselves in it.

But one thing is clear to me: if a data visualization is without context, or approachability, or apparent meaning, it loses value. A parade of numbers is just that, especially if the audience lacks knowledge of the subject. That audience needs stories.

When a designer can simply choose a particular type of chart from hundreds of different types and apply it to a dataset, digital engineers have removed human thinking. Yes, it means that data visualizers can now deal with huge bundles of numbers, but somehow in that process, helpful, reader-friendly, representational images are exiled. It's easy to let the computer think for you—it's seductive—and it is harder to draw recognizable things instead of letting a program draw elegant, abstract swooping lines for you.

Many data visualizers would like what they do to be considered a branch of science. They want their work to be, or appear to be, scientific, because that suggests authority. (The cynic on my shoulder whispers that if you call yourself an authority, you can charge more for what you do.) I think that infographic artists and designers, as well as strict data visualizers, should approach scientific and other subjects from their own viewpoint, more straightforwardly, as an outside reporter. And while the subject may be serious, the approach to it can take a lighter, less cold and analytic, turn.

At the very least, let's ditch jargon—that special exclusionary language that every profession uses to keep a wall around their private club. Part of the job of the joyful infografista is to use clear, jargon-free explanations.

Some of the smartest designers of data visualizations work for newspapers (and their websites) around the world. I have great admiration for the work they do, and having been a weekly deadline jockey myself, I understand the pressures they are under to do it on a daily basis.

Their ability to find, then sort through, and then select the most appropriate form in which to display the data, is justly celebrated. *The New York Times, The Washington Post, The Financial Times, The Guardian,* and *The South China Morning Post,* to mention just a few, kept us splendidly up-to-date and informed throughout the data-heavy Covid 19 pandemic.

As noted at the start of this history, infographics in the past have been dominated by men. In the 21st century, there's a cohort of women making joyful infographics. And they are not afraid to ditch the computer and use their hands. (Now that really is digital!)

Here are just a few:

Megan Jaegerman did largely pictorial, black and white charts for *The New York Times* from 1990 to 1998, and she gave the 'old gray lady' a delightfully lighter touch.

Stephanie Posavec and **Giorgia Lupi** wrote a postcard to each other across the Atlantic for 52 weeks, hand-charting their personal lives in intricate detail. Their project, *Dear Data,* is now housed in the Museum of Modern Art.

Separately, **Stephanie,** this time with a different collaborator, **Miriam Quick**, has produced a terrific children's book *(see it in the science chapter).* And **Giorgia,** a partner at the design firm Pentagram, has created several data visualization projects that emphasize people first and data later, urging us all to 'speak data' along with whatever other language we speak.

Eleanor Lutz is a graphics editor at *The New York Times.* Her elegant and clever science diagrams make you want to immediately read and study them. **Mona Chalabi** is a passionate illustrator, data journalist and producer, whose writing and art has appeared in the *New Yorker, Five Thirty Eight, The Guardian,* and *The New York Times.*

Paula Scher, another partner at Pentagram, is not known as an information designer, but her huge, intricately hand-drawn and painted maps suggest she might be one at heart. Her maps certainly suggest a new direction for cartography. A simplified version of Paula's map of Africa can be seen on supermarket shelves *(right)*; it's part of the packaging for Fonio, an ancient West African grain, and it's a perfect, friendly infographic for this book: the maker's name, Yolélé, means 'let the good times roll.'

Next: Nine ways to make your infographics joyful.

Nine ways to make your graphics joyful

FIRST WAY **Know Your Audience**

You can't make joyful infographics, or any *useful* infographics, if you don't know your audience. I mean the audience for the particular job you are working on. I do believe that everyone—including those with specialist knowledge of their subject—can benefit from a friendly graphic helping hand, but you shouldn't talk down to scientists, for example, by over-simplifying their work. When you are explaining scientific concepts to non-scientists—that's different. In both cases, making the information clear is the goal. By the way, I much prefer the word *clarifying* to *simplifying*. More to come on that, later.

So, ask questions about your audience.

First, the obvious one: **who is this job for?** Adults? Teenagers? People who really know their subject (i.e., those scientists)? Just women? Mostly men? Children, before they can read? Do you think who's reading makes a difference? It does.

Do some in your audience not speak English? (Or a language that's not the one you are using.) Wouldn't you like to reach that part of your readership? Recently, for a pamphlet I designed to explain food scrap recycling, the project organizers knew that many people in the community were Hispanic. They wondered if I would make a version with the text in Spanish? Of course! It was both a practical and a friendly thing to do. And it didn't take long. But designers beware: Spanish runs longer than English!

What about blind people? There are Braille keyboards, and web-based voiced descriptions—similar to spoken subtitles on streamed movies and TV shows. Screen readers can translate text for users (your web pages must be specifically designed to make use of them). Tactile, Braille-like graphics are good for understanding spatial relationships within data, but they are very expensive to produce. In 1837, a beautiful *Atlas of the United States Printed for the Use of the Blind* was produced in an edition of 50 copies with embossed maps and text. There's a copy in the David Rumsey Map Collection—see it online. Braille itself was invented in 1825, but the system wasn't used in the *Atlas* because it hadn't been universally adopted at that time.

People with red-green
color deficiency see
these colors...   ...like this

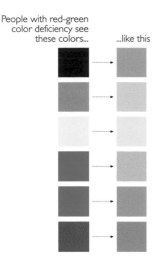

And those who have **Color Vision Disability**? (It's usually referred to as color blindness, but that term does not accurately describe the problem.) The most common difficulty for the 350 million people worldwide with CVD is seeing the difference between red and green. The chart on the left shows what some colors look like if you have CVD.

Despite what might seem like inconveniences for designers, we all should make the effort to create graphics that are accessible to as many people as possible. The effort is nothing compared to the inconvenience of the sufferers. Think of it like this: paying attention to the needs of your audience is similar to being sensitive about guests' food allergies; in fact, perhaps *guests* is a better word than *audience*. Imagine that you are having a data conversation with your guest readers, and that some of them cannot understand you. Organizations currently engaged in further research into accessibility for everyone, not just the visually impaired are listed at the back of the book.

Two things about the whole subject of the audience. We have to be realistic. First, we may not know exactly who our guests are, and second, not knowing who they are might mean that we play safe and by making things too simple and straightforward. But remember that many of us pretend to know more about a subject than we really do. We nod approvingly during a conversation so as not to admit ignorance, letting on that we are ill-equipped to be part of the conversation. Few of us say *'I don't know.'*

If our guest audience doesn't understand us, it's not their fault; it's our graphic. Making things clear is not the same as treating readers like children, who understand much more than we give them credit for, anyway. If they don't understand—from about age four—they can look up anything they want on the web. Does that argue that we don't have to pay any attention to who is reading our stuff? No, that is not the point of joyful infographics! The point is to engage our audience (readers, users, viewers, guests) so that they don't have to puzzle it out.

 **Visual Prosody**

Prosody is the pattern of stress and intonation in language—inflection. I didn't know what prosody meant, either, but I thought it would be OK to have a word in the book that I had to look up. Prosody is what makes reading and listening to words enjoyable, and holds many keys to understanding what someone is saying. Does the sound of a spoken sentence go up a little at the end? In print, there's a question mark to let you know you are posing a question. In speech, it's that little upward lilt. By extension, visual prosody is how you say something visually—how you present data. Visual prosody is really what this book is all about. It seems obvious to say that the way you express data visually can make an infographic joyful—or awful. But obvious is good. Let's see: take a paragraph about a set of numbers; list the numbers; then arrange them into a table; then chart the numbers; then do something with the chart. It's all the same information, told in different forms.

Visual prosody in action: 8 ways to 'say' the data

1. PLAIN TEXT

Sales Report
For the first five months of 2022, starting with $3 million in January, sales steadily climbed to $10 million.

2022	Sales
Jan	$3,000,000
Feb	$4,000,000
Mar	$5,500,000
Apr	$8,000,000
May	$10,000,000

2. TABLE

3a. BAR CHART

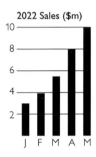

3b. BAR CHART
Putting the exact quantities above each bar eliminates the need for grid lines.

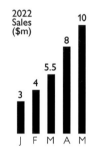

4. LINE CHART
Line charts track one thing (here, dollars) over time, so it might be a better choice than a bar chart.

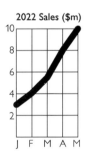

5. SLOPE CHART
Because the line essentially goes up without any big advances or drops, you can let it jump from the first to the last number.

6. Wait, it's a catfood company?

Wrap the slope chart round a simple tin can. (Don't overdo the detail)

But this doesn't look like the right sort of can for petfood.

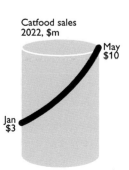

8. Most petfood comes in cans shaped more like this. So here's the joyful 'voice.' Please don't let the illustration get in the way of the data; and do respect the baseline.

You say tomayto, and I say tomarto.

Years ago, I picked up this card in an old schoolhouse-turned-restaurant in Montana. It took me a little time to understand that the name, when spoken out loud, was 'Caffay,' and not 'Carfay,' which is the way I am used to pronouncing 'calf.' The almost non-design of the card was exactly right for this tiny, out-of-the-way place,

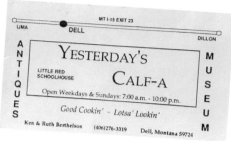

with its minimal map and directions at the top, and the punny name. Perfect prosody! If you play 'I Spy' towns that have the same name as computer companies (a strange game, to be sure!), head up to Dell, Montana.*

Context, Comparisons and Connections

Everything can be understood better when you see it next to something you already know or understand. If you upend the *Queen Mary 2* ocean liner and stand her next to the Empire State Building in New York, you see how big the ship is. (And if you are a pasenger you can see the building as you pull into the dock.)

How do other countries (and the moon) measure up to the US?

Here's the same map of the US compared to the continent of Africa.

---

* I called one of the current owners of the Calf-A, Shanna Lamb, who, with her husband EJ, bought it in April 2021. It's now called the Old Schoolhouse Café, and is open from 8am to 3pm, and closed on Wednesday and Thursday.

Illustrator Peter Grundy compared the size of Nelson's Column in London to the great Admiral's ship *Victory,* and included a double-decker bus and the nuclear-powered submarine *Dreadnought,* perfectly fitting them all into a stamp commissioned by Royal Mail to commemorate the 1805 Battle of Trafalgar, *(below).*

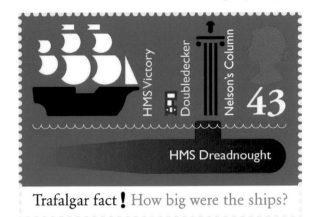

Trafalgar fact ! How big were the ships?

Nelson's Column in Trafalgar Square also appears in this old postcard, *(right)*—compared to the original *Queen Mary.* New contexts, better understanding.

Noticing an unexpected connection between two people is a good exercise in understanding the power of context. For example, the satirist Jonathan Swift was living in Dublin, Ireland, at the time that Frederick Handel was composing *Messiah.* Dublin, a relatively small city, was a center of music and the arts in the mid-1700s, so it's likely that Swift and Handel met, especially since Swift, who was Dean of St. Patrick's Cathedral at the time, did not want his two cathedral choirs to be part of the first public performance of *Messiah.* That took place in a *musick* hall, which to Swift was a profane place. I'm imagining the lively conversation between the acerbic satirist and the ex-pat with a heavy German accent.

And those two guys mentioned as influences in chapter one? Eadweard Muybridge and the slightly older Edward Lear were alive at the same time. Before Muybridge emigrated to the US, I'd like to think that he and Lear sat in a London coffee house in 1852 discussing Dickens' new novel *Bleak House* or Harriet Beecher Stowe's *Uncle Tom's Cabin* which were both published that year. Or, a year later, arguing for or against compulsory smallpox vaccination in Britain. Lear could also boast about the private drawing lessons he gave to the 27-year-old Queen Victoria. Someone should make a movie. *(Edward and Eadweard?)*

If you let your mind wander away from the literal to the possible, all sorts of connections pop up, and that'll make your graphics interestingly different. Brian Haynes, the art director who gave me great uncle George's boat drawings as reference for a job, used this principle in his magazine design: he included everything that interested him about the subject at hand; he made connections and comparisons, with quotes, illustrations, photos, charts, and maps.

Information graphic designers are often taught to strip out any fun for the sake of clarity, or because critics say they are obscuring the message with unnecessary bits and pieces. But if a connection or a comparison throws extra light on the subject, I'm with Brian: include it!

It's the same with my favorite TV shows: *Seinfeld, Curb Your Enthusiasm, Ted Lasso*. The seemingly obscure references in the scripts of these shows come at you so quickly that unless you rewind and look and listen again, you'll miss them. It's the richness of their inclusion that makes viewing so pleasurable. I know, I know, TV sitcoms are meant to be entertaining—and that isn't the point of infographics. But including a level of meaning and interest, beneath the main message, is a good example to follow. Both TV sitcoms and information graphics have to strike a balance between fun and a clear storyline.

Most people are mixed up about big numbers.

Politicians and pundits don't help; they throw numbers around without context or explanation. A billion-dollar budget—that's big. A trillion? Well, it's bigger, but how much bigger? Just saying a thousand times bigger is not helpful. Show it!

We'll start with a smaller number: how 'big' is a million dollars? It will fit into the kind of bag you are allowed to carry onto a plane. A billion dollars? You'll need an 8.5ft cube, 615 square

If you had a million dollars in $100 bills, you could carry it in this bag

15 inches

(8 inches deep)

10 inches

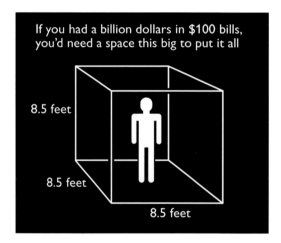

If you had a billion dollars in $100 bills, you'd need a space this big to put it all

8.5 feet

8.5 feet

8.5 feet

feet—basically a cupboard—to contain it (again, in $100 bills). And for a trillion dollars? The space needed to house that pile of money in $100 bills is 384,000 square feet. Here's where finding a relatable context for your audience is important. You can't compare that much to an everyday thing like a suitcase or a cupboard. Let's say you are giving a talk in New York; 384,000 square feet is the size of the main hall at Grand Central Terminal, *(top right)*. This will give most New Yorkers a context from their own city. If your speech is in Washington DC, a trillion dollars in $100 bills would go a third of the way up the Washington Monument. The DC audience (and a lot of tourists) would then have a good mental picture.

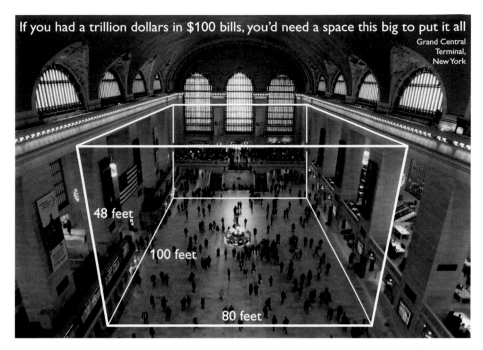

If you had a trillion dollars in $100 bills, you'd need a space this big to put it all

Grand Central Terminal, New York

48 feet

100 feet

80 feet

Why do we visualize a government budget as one big lump? What's the point, apart from WOW! The US budget's billions are split into smaller sums that come back to us in the form of childcare, Medicare, education, pensions, roads, bridges, and battleships. Although still huge, those smaller numbers are more relevant to our everyday life. Yet graphic comparisons are often made to the overall amount. Why? Because it gets immediate attention; those important details can wait, we will show them after grabbing our audience. Joyful Infographics start out as the big picture, an introduction to the small print, which itself comes later.

Bringing data down to a human scale, indeed using the human body itself in some way, makes for a good relatable context when explaining facts. After all, we know our bodies, we carry them around with us. All we really know about the Empire State Building, or the Eiffel Tower, is that they are tall landmarks that we may or may not have seen, or know much about at all.

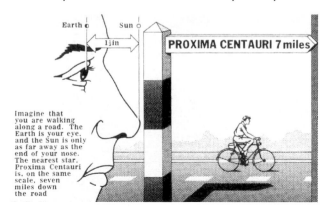

Earth o   Sun o

1½in

PROXIMA CENTAURI 7 miles

Imagine that you are walking along a road. The Earth is your eye, and the Sun is only as far away as the end of your nose. The nearest star, Proxima Centauri is, on the same scale, seven miles down the road

For a Radio Times feature about the future of really long-distance space travel, I tried to help readers visualize immense distances, (left).

The light from our sun takes eight minutes to reach us. Light from the nearest star takes four and a half years.

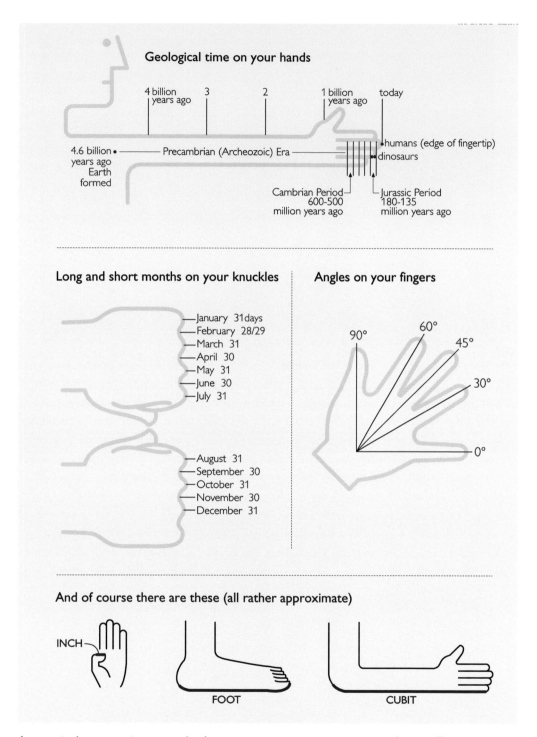

Geological time on your hands

4 billion years ago   3   2   1 billion years ago   today

4.6 billion years ago Earth formed • ——— Precambrian (Archeozoic) Era ———

• humans (edge of fingertip)
◄ dinosaurs

Cambrian Period
600-500
million years ago

Jurassic Period
180-135
million years ago

Long and short months on your knuckles

—January 31days
—February 28/29
—March 31
—April 30
—May 31
—June 30
—July 31

—August 31
—September 30
—October 31
—November 30
—December 31

Angles on your fingers

90°   60°   45°   30°   0°

And of course there are these (all rather approximate)

INCH

FOOT

CUBIT

Anatomical mnemonics—your body as context—easy ways to remember stuff.

I found these on the web in various styles, uncredited. Here they are redrawn for consistency.

Middlebury recycles a ton of stuff.

Actually, quite a few tons. To give you an idea of how much, we've compared what we recycle to the weight of various animals and vehicles.

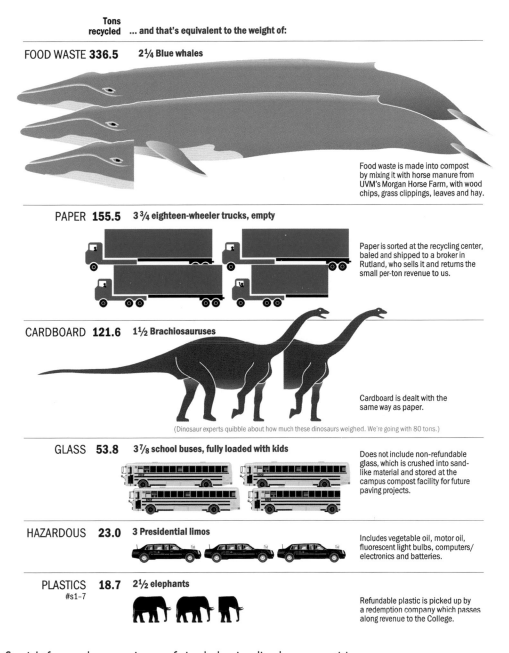

	Tons recycled	... and that's equivalent to the weight of:

FOOD WASTE 336.5 2¼ Blue whales

Food waste is made into compost by mixing it with horse manure from UVM's Morgan Horse Farm, with wood chips, grass clippings, leaves and hay.

PAPER 155.5 3¾ eighteen-wheeler trucks, empty

Paper is sorted at the recycling center, baled and shipped to a broker in Rutland, who sells it and returns the small per-ton revenue to us.

CARDBOARD 121.6 1½ Brachiosauruses

Cardboard is dealt with the same way as paper.

(Dinosaur experts quibble about how much these dinosaurs weighed. We're going with 80 tons.)

GLASS 53.8 3⅞ school buses, fully loaded with kids

Does not include non-refundable glass, which is crushed into sand-like material and stored at the campus compost facility for future paving projects.

HAZARDOUS 23.0 3 Presidential limos

Includes vegetable oil, motor oil, fluorescent light bulbs, computers/electronics and batteries.

PLASTICS 18.7 2½ elephants
#s1–7

Refundable plastic is picked up by a redemption company which passes along revenue to the College.

Straightforward comparisons of size help visualize large quantities.

Above, all the stuff recycled by Middlebury College. (Art Director: Pamela Fogg)

The whales are nice, but you don't have to force every comparison to be with something you can visualize. For our 2019 book *Mortality*—basically a collection of infographics—Richard Saul Wurman and I needed to show a lot of data, but we wanted to be sure that each set of numbers had an anchoring context. What's the murder rate in the US? We compared it to the rate in England and Wales. (Both graph lines, *(below),* represented homicides per 100,000 people per year, so the difference in population was eliminated.) It's an example of a difficult subject treated with restraint. That line crawling across the bottom of the chart gave us in America a clear view of our problem—a context for those deadly numbers at the top.

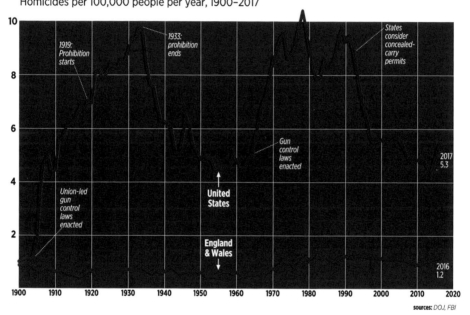

What's the murder rate in the US? ...and compared to the rate in England & Wales
Homicides per 100,000 people per year, 1900–2017

1919: Prohibition starts

1933: prohibition ends

States consider concealed-carry permits

Gun control laws enacted

2017
5.3

Union-led gun control laws enacted

United States

England & Wales

2016
1.2

sources: DOJ, FBI

How many people died in World War II? The numbers are even more horrifying when you see them next to other modern wars, *(below).* You probably didn't know those numbers in detail, but shown like this they give meaning to each other—in other words, a context.

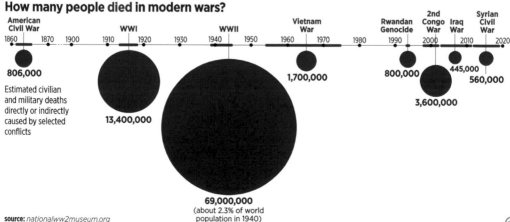

How many people died in modern wars?

American Civil War	WWI	WWII	Vietnam War	Rwandan Genocide	2nd Congo War	Iraq War	Syrian Civil War

1860   1870   1900   1910   1920   1930   1940   1950   1960   1970   1980   1990   2000   2010   2020

806,000

Estimated civilian and military deaths directly or indirectly caused by selected conflicts

13,400,000

1,700,000

800,000

445,000

560,000

3,600,000

69,000,000
(about 2.3% of world population in 1940)

source: *nationalww2museum.org*

Charts about death can hardly be called joyful, but even deadly subjects should be approachable for the audience. You don't need to shock readers with dead bodies. Leaving out such obvious images doesn't sanitize the data, or make the subject more palatable. Let context—additional data— do the work of helping readers understand the numbers.

Do I have to draw you a picture?

You can suggest a context without using a graphic at all. In July 2021, a tiny silverpoint drawing sold at auction for a huge sum. Just how tiny was the drawing? *The New York Times* headline put it perfectly: 'A Leonardo da Vinci the size of a Post-it sells for $12.2 million.' (See earlier, that's 12 carry-on bags!)

Or here's Gail Collins, writing about robocalls in the same newspaper, and giving a nice human context '[there were] an estimated 45.9 billion robocalls in 2020. That's about 1,455 a second. In the time it takes you to blink, 1,455 people are being robo-ed.'

In a demonstration to show how much toothpaste is used every day by people in the US, I rolled out a thin strip of black paper on the floor across the stage in front of me. I squeezed out a long white line of toothpaste onto it. One end of the line represented Los Angeles, the other, New York. The point was that this length of toothpaste was the daily amount of toothpaste used in the US. (I estimated the amount, 2,450 miles, based on a sample of colleagues' bathroom habits.) But after doing this elaborate performance a few times, I realized that I didn't need to be so theatrical. Instead, I asked the audience to close their eyes, imagine a map of America, color it black, and then 'draw' a white line across it from coast to coast. That's a visual of the amount of toothpaste used every day in the US. It was right there in their minds' eye—no graphic was needed.

When we don't think about our readers, we miss a chance to help them by putting facts into an understandable context. The Heritage Foundation maintains a database of mail-in voting numbers and found that fraud in the two decades of elections before 2020 'was about 0.00006% of total votes cast.' Although that's clearly very small, it's not a friendly number. I wonder if it would it have made the slightest difference to anyone's understanding if the number quoted had been 0.0006%? (Look closely.) About 250 million mail-in votes were cast during the 20 years from 2000 to 2019, while the number of people who voted illegally in that period was just over 1,200. Isn't 1,200 votes a more graspable, human number than 0.00006%? All those zeroes tell you that voter fraud is very rare. When you state the number as it relates to living people, you can see it's a really, really rare.

Using relatable context is not only a concept that fosters understanding within an infographic, it's also useful to think about *where* the graphic appears—when the context itself is surprising. This can be as simple as making your graphic look like a comic strip—with speech balloons instead of text blocks—and running it in a conventionally laid out magazine or paper. An unusual context—the out-of-context context as it were—is what makes the information visible. For instance, in presentations, I've tried to demonstrate how far world-class athletes can jump. Hotel conference rooms aren't the usual context for the long jump. First, I measure 29+ feet on the floor in front of the audience, then step back, make a short run-up and jump… about 7 feet! Embarrassed, I walk to the marker at the other end of the measured 29 feet to reveal the athletes' feat. *Their* feet didn't touch the ground on the way there from the take off board. Spectators at the Olympics expect jumpers to do amazing things, but indoors, in the confines of a conference room, you can really experience how far a superhuman can jump.

Here are more examples of visual context.

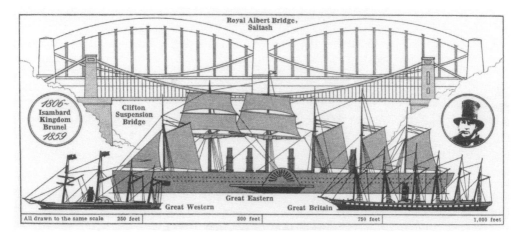

For the Radio Times, this graphic accompanied a program listing about Brunel, showing his amazing 19th century engineering feats, in scale to each other.

Another diagram for the program pages of the Radio Times, this one giving English viewers a familiar height comparison for the Olympic ski jump. (Jumpers didn't wear helmets in 1972 at the Sapporo Games.)

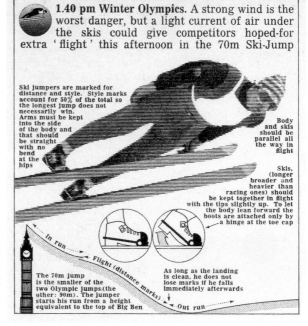

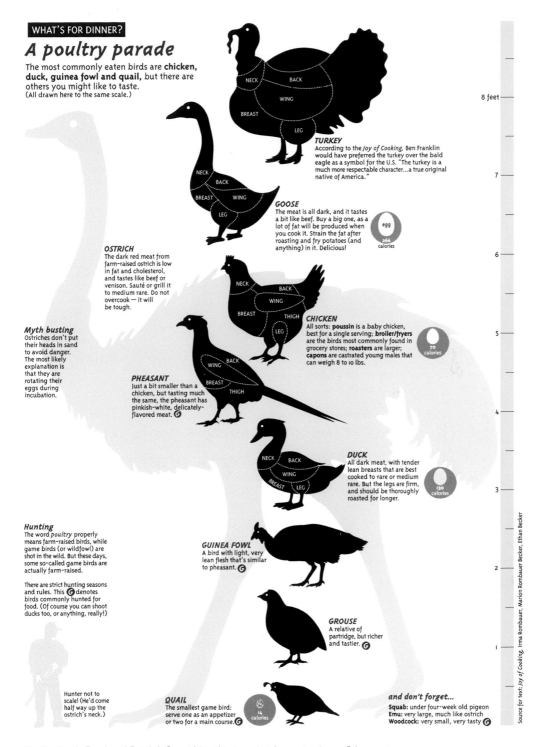

WHAT'S FOR DINNER?

A poultry parade

The most commonly eaten birds are **chicken, duck, guinea fowl and quail,** but there are others you might like to taste.
(All drawn here to the same scale.)

TURKEY
According to the *Joy of Cooking,* Ben Franklin would have preferred the turkey over the bald eagle as a symbol for the U.S. "The turkey is a much more respectable character...a true original native of America."

GOOSE
The meat is all dark, and it tastes a bit like beef. Buy a big one, as a lot of fat will be produced when you cook it. Strain the fat after roasting and fry potatoes (and anything) in it. Delicious!

egg
366 calories

OSTRICH
The dark red meat from farm-raised ostrich is low in fat and cholesterol, and tastes like beef or venison. Sauté or grill it to medium rare. Do not overcook — it will be tough.

Myth busting
Ostriches don't put their heads in sand to avoid danger. The most likely explanation is that they are rotating their eggs during incubation.

CHICKEN
All sorts: **poussin** is a baby chicken, best for a single serving; **broiler/fryers** are the birds most commonly found in grocery stores; **roasters** are larger; **capons** are castrated young males that can weigh 8 to 10 lbs.

70 calories

PHEASANT
Just a bit smaller than a chicken, but tasting much the same, the pheasant has pinkish-white, delicately-flavored meat. Ⓖ

DUCK
All dark meat, with tender lean breasts that are best cooked to rare or medium rare. But the legs are firm, and should be thoroughly roasted for longer.

130 calories

Hunting
The word *poultry* properly means farm-raised birds, while game birds (or wildfowl) are shot in the wild. But these days, some so-called game birds are actually farm-raised.

There are strict hunting seasons and rules. This Ⓖ denotes birds commonly hunted for food. (Of course you can shoot ducks too, or anything, really!)

GUINEA FOWL
A bird with light, very lean flesh that's similar to pheasant. Ⓖ

GROUSE
A relative of partridge, but richer and tastier. Ⓖ

Hunter not to scale! (He'd come half way up the ostrich's neck.)

QUAIL
The smallest game bird: serve one as an appetizer or two for a main course. Ⓖ

14 calories

and don't forget...
Squab: under four-week old pigeon
Emu: very large, much like ostrich
Woodcock: very small, very tasty Ⓖ

8 feet

7

6

5

4

3

2

1

Source for text: *Joy of Cooking,* Irma Rombauer, Marion Rombauer Becker, Ethan Becker

For Taschen's Food and Drink Infographics, this is a simple comparison of the most commonly eaten birds (and their eggs) all drawn to the same scale. (Keep the hunter image in mind: he first appeared in a graphic about Lyme disease, included in the science chapter. It's OK to recycle your stuff! ⊕

*In our book Mortality,
Richard Saul Wurman
and I tried two ways to
show the same info.*

*More people are afraid
of sharks than mosquitos
which the top graphic
seems to confirm—at
least graphically.*

*But far more people die
from mosquito-borne
malaria than from shark
attacks, and that fact is
more obvious in the lower
graphic. (We printed both
versions in the book.)*

What are you more afraid of, sharks?...

**Worldwide, sharks
killed 5 people in 2017**
(as a result of
88 unprovoked
attacks).

5
deaths
annually

**Where the attacks
occurred.** Most shark *bites*
take place in Florida, but
the average annual fatality
there is less than one. The
most **fatal** shark attacks
occur in Australia.

• **attacks in 2017**
• fatalities

source: *International Shark Attack File*

What are you more afraid of, sharks?...

Worldwide, sharks killed 5 people in 2017.
(As a result of 88 unprovoked attacks).

*Yes, it's the same
information as
on the previous
pages, but here
with a different
viewpoint.*

5
deaths
annually

**Where the attacks
occurred.** Most shark
bites take place in
Florida, but the
average annual fatality
there is less than one.
The most **fatal** shark
attacks occur in
Australia.

• **attacks in 2017**
• fatalities

source: *International Shark Attack File*

...or mosquitos?

The World Health Organization estimates that more than a million people die from malaria every year.
Female mosquitos carry the parasite that causes malaria.
More people have been killed by mosquitos than in all wars in history.

deaths
annually

Half the world's population is at risk of malaria. Children under five are the most likely group to be infected by a mosquito carrying the disease, and 70% of total deaths are from this age group.

source: *WHO*

...or mosquitos?

The World Health Organization estimates that more than a million people die from malaria every year.
Female mosquitos carry the parasite that causes the disease.
More people have been killed by mosquitos than in all wars in history.

deaths
annually

Half the world's population is at risk of malaria. Children under five are the most likely group to be infected by a mosquito carrying the disease, and 70% of total deaths are from this age group.

source: *WHO*

⬤ Metaphor

Along with clichés, I've had an on-again, off-again affair with metaphors. Infographics have their own built-in metaphors: pie charts, fever lines, table of figures, family trees. (I suppose some families do plant a tree and call it a family tree, but you know what I mean.) Writers use metaphors with a natural ease: *'All the world's a stage, and all the men and women merely players'*—Shakespeare in *As You Like It*. Or *'You ain't nothin' but a hound dog'* famously sung by Elvis Presley in 1956, but originally written by Jerry Leiber and Mike Stoller 4 years earlier for 'Big Mama' Thornton. (It made more sense sung by a woman.) I used to ask writers at *Time* what they thought would make a good graphic for the article they were working on. When they said 'I don't know, I'm a word person,' I wondered what a word person might look like, *right?).* But then they'll say: 'Well, it's the tail wagging the dog.' OK, I'll try that.

Just in case you are not sure, a metaphor is a figure of speech that's not true in a literal way, but is an implied comparison. *You are an angel*—metaphor. Metaphor's cousin, simile, is slightly different. *You sing like an angel*—that's a simile. Similes use *like* or *as* to draw comparisons.

Visual metaphors can come uncomfortably close to cliché—yes, I know I said earlier that for me clichés are obvious truths. At *Time* magazine I made a list of images that I hoped editors would stop asking me to draw, because they were overdone. Today, I avoid these ones in graphics: rainbows, roller coasters, mountain ranges, Hokusai's *Wave*, Grant Wood's *American Gothic* (I've used both in the past, but now I think they should just be Art), mazes, horizons, precipices, ladders, the *Monopoly* board, telescopes (for anything in the future), icebergs (as in tip of; but oooh, do you see what's underwater?), hourglasses (time's always running out), banana peels.

Some metaphors have eye-opening origins: when a renaissance aristocrat commissioned a portrait, the artist would charge extra if an arm and a leg were visible in the finished painting. Other metaphors have a straightforward background: that deadline we either fear or rely on to get the job done; it was the perimeter around a prison, where inmates would be shot if they went beyond it.

I suggest you use visual metaphors with care. If you draw a roller coaster to align exactly with the points on a line chart, and title it *A bumpy ride* (I've done this, too), it's a metaphor alright, but it's too obvious as a visual and verbal comparison. Instead, try to find a metaphor that adds insight to the information, and isn't just an illustration to make a chart look interesting.

As I mentioned in the history chapter, Robert Chapin's maps for *Time* included drawn metaphors. His preliminary sketch *(below)* for the 'Body Blow' WWII map, shows that he was not only a cartographer, but also a fine draughtsman. Part of Chapin's successful map is the context in which it appears: a respected magazine article about a deadly war.

Here, context and metaphor work perfectly together.

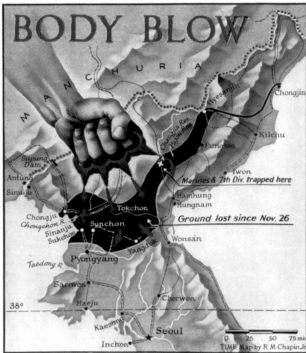

I had cataract surgery in 2019. At a follow-up consultation, the doctor described cataracts in a way I had not heard before. The lens in your eye floats inside something like a transparent M&M (or a Smartie in England). The 'chocolate' inside this shell is what clouds your vision, and that's what the surgeon scrapes out, before inserting a new man-made lens. It was an effective, and strangely comforting explanation.

Actual size.
(The purple one
is a Smartie.)

Rejecting the metaphor

Sometimes it's good to think hard about whether an accepted metaphor is appropriate. The newspaper *USA Today* asked a number of designers to rethink the official US Food Pyramid—recommendations for how much of what foods you should eat to be healthy.

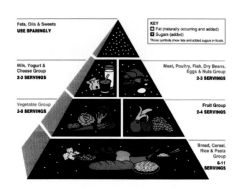

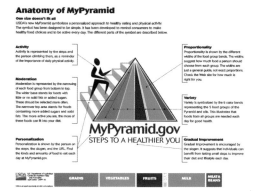

The original USDA pyramid, *(above),* was redesigned in 2005, *(above, right),* in an effort to make it more personal. Unfortunately, the spiky figure climbing up the side of the pyramid gets a shock on arrival at the top, since the six food groups have tapered to a point, leaving nothing to eat at all. Also, the tapering contradicts the caption which says that the more exercise you do, the more food you can eat. At least the original (black) graphic had suggested quantities, and it showed the food groups distributed according to official dietary recommendations of the time. It was this new diagram that spurred *USA Today* to ask designers for their ideas.

I started, as I always do, with mind-wandering sketches, including a thought about whether I could construct a face like the famous paintings made out of fruit and vegetables by Giuseppe Arcimboldo in the 16th century. But that seemed forced, so I quickly turned to diagramming the recommended proportions of the major food groups, which were simple. I briefly tried to keep a human in the picture, *(below),* but gave that up, too.

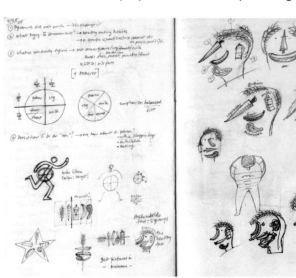

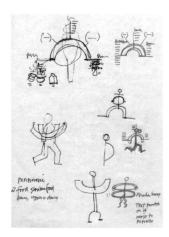

I never considered reorganizing the pyramid, partly because it didn't work as a good metaphor, and partly because I felt there should be a complete change to help people examine their diets afresh. My final design *(above)* reflected the USDA recommended dietary proportions: vegetables, grains and dairy all at 25%; 15% for fruit; 10% for meat. I made a small logo, too.

In 2010, five years after this appeared in *USA Today,* I was invited to join a group of nutritionists, marketing experts, and infographic designers at a White House meeting to discuss a renewed initiative to promote official dietary guidelines. (I was disappointed that the meeting didn't take place at the White House itself! It was across the street.) In 2011, the resulting icon was announced. It was gratifying to see what the government's designers came up with—MyPlate.

On the following pages are more examples of visual metaphors.

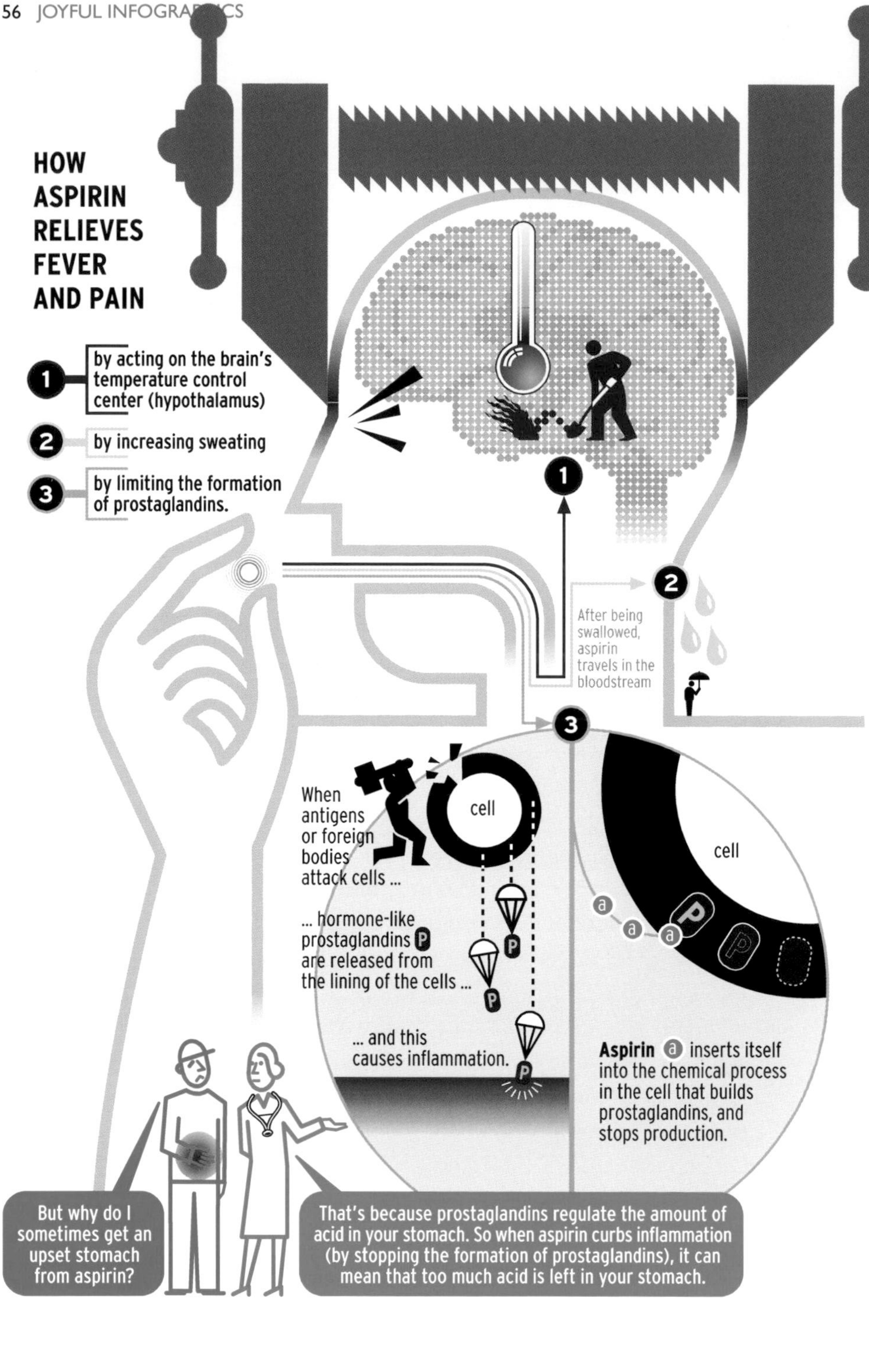

HOW ASPIRIN RELIEVES FEVER AND PAIN

1 by acting on the brain's temperature control center (hypothalamus)

2 by increasing sweating

3 by limiting the formation of prostaglandins.

After being swallowed, aspirin travels in the bloodstream

When antigens or foreign bodies attack cells ...

... hormone-like prostaglandins **P** are released from the lining of the cells ...

... and this causes inflammation.

cell

cell

Aspirin (a) inserts itself into the chemical process in the cell that builds prostaglandins, and stops production.

But why do I sometimes get an upset stomach from aspirin?

That's because prostaglandins regulate the amount of acid in your stomach. So when aspirin curbs inflammation (by stopping the formation of prostaglandins), it can mean that too much acid is left in your stomach.

What did I say about clichés? Oh, well! Here are three graphics that use the same idea. The one above, for Attaché magazine, also uses the idea of a 'Greek chorus' of little people at the bottom, adding info to the graphic. (More about this in Labelling, number seven in this chapter.)

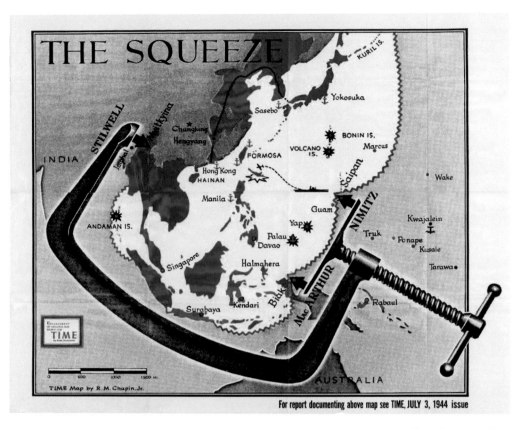

THE SQUEEZE

TIME Map by R.M.Chapin.Jr.

For report documenting above map see TIME, JULY 3, 1944 issue

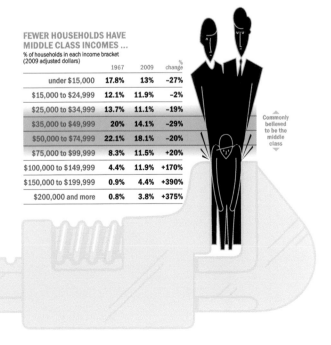

FEWER HOUSEHOLDS HAVE MIDDLE CLASS INCOMES ...
% of households in each income bracket
(2009 adjusted dollars)

	1967	2009	% change
under $15,000	17.8%	13%	-27%
$15,000 to $24,999	12.1%	11.9%	-2%
$25,000 to $34,999	13.7%	11.1%	-19%
$35,000 to $49,999	20%	14.1%	-29%
$50,000 to $74,999	22.1%	18.1%	-20%
$75,000 to $99,999	8.3%	11.5%	+20%
$100,000 to $149,999	4.4%	11.9%	+170%
$150,000 to $199,999	0.9%	4.4%	+390%
$200,000 and more	0.8%	3.8%	+375%

Commonly
believed
to be the
middle
class

Chapin's maps-with-metaphors for Time magazine during WW2 always thrill me. Look at the way his metal clamp is so obviously 'outside' the map—as though it's just been placed on top of the map after it was finished.

*An uncomfortable detail from a graphic about household incomes from American History magazine.
(Art Director Rudy Hoglund.)*

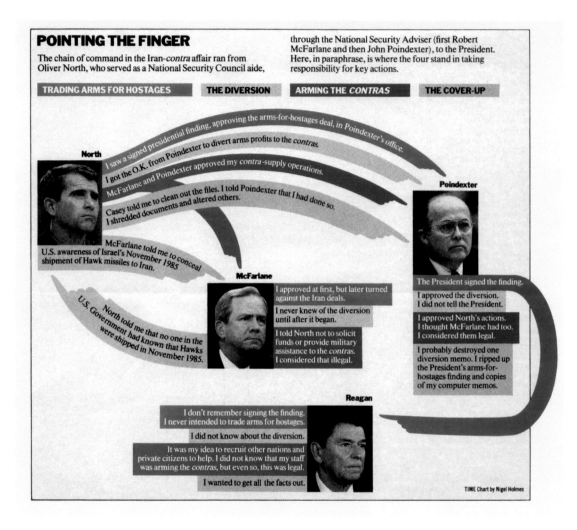

POINTING THE FINGER

The chain of command in the Iran-*contra* affair ran from Oliver North, who served as a National Security Council aide, through the National Security Adviser (first Robert McFarlane and then John Poindexter), to the President. Here, in paraphrase, is where the four stand in taking responsibility for key actions.

TRADING ARMS FOR HOSTAGES   **THE DIVERSION**   **ARMING THE *CONTRAS***   **THE COVER-UP**

North

I saw a signed presidential finding, approving the arms-for-hostages deal, in Poindexter's office.

I got the O.K. from Poindexter to divert arms profits to the *contras*.

McFarlane and Poindexter approved my *contra*-supply operations.

Casey told me to clean out the files. I told Poindexter that I had done so. I shredded documents and altered others.

McFarlane told me to conceal U.S. awareness of Israel's November 1985 shipment of Hawk missiles to Iran.

North told me that no one in the U.S. Government had known that Hawks were shipped in November 1985.

McFarlane

I approved at first, but later turned against the Iran deals.

I never knew of the diversion until after it began.

I told North not to solicit funds or provide military assistance to the *contras*. I considered that illegal.

Poindexter

The President signed the finding.

I approved the diversion. I did not tell the President.

I approved North's actions. I thought McFarlane had too. I considered them legal.

I probably destroyed one diversion memo. I ripped up the President's arms-for-hostages finding and copies of my computer memos.

Reagan

I don't remember signing the finding. I never intended to trade arms for hostages.

I did not know about the diversion.

It was my idea to recruit other nations and private citizens to help. I did not know that my staff was arming the *contras*, but even so, this was legal.

I wanted to get all the facts out.

TIME Chart by Nigel Holmes

Perhaps my favorite graphic from Time magazine, from 1987, making the type go exactly where I wanted it to, and showing the ultimate in political buck-passing, followed by Reagan's denial that he knew anything.

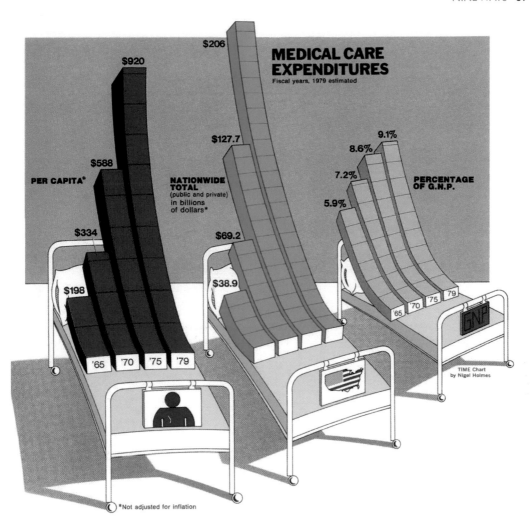

MEDICAL CARE EXPENDITURES
Fiscal years, 1979 estimated

$920

$588

$334

$198

PER CAPITA*

$206

$127.7

$69.2

$38.9

NATIONWIDE
TOTAL
(public and private)
in billions
of dollars*

9.1%

8.6%

7.2%

5.9%

PERCENTAGE
OF G.N.P.

'65   '70   '75   '79

65   '70   '75   79

GNP

TIME Chart
by Nigel Holmes

*Not adjusted for inflation

In 1979, I made the costs of
medical care sit up in hospital
beds. An acceptable graphic
method today? I think so.
(Art director Walter Bernard.)

An Illustration for the New
Yorker about dissonance in
Dvorak's music, composed
using the 12-tone scale. The
scowling face is made from
musical notation marks. I've
used that old engraving
of ears a few times.
(Art director Owen Philllips.)

FIFTH WAY Simplicity and Clarity

In lectures, I often show a slide with one word on it: 'simplify.' While I'm explaining that simplifying information might be taken to mean dumbing it down, the word on the screen morphs into 'clarify.'

So, don't *simplify* your graphics; instead, use them to *clarify* the information. Just semantics, you say? It's a fair point—when you clarify something, you may well be simplifying parts of it—but I still don't want people to mistake simplifying for dumbing down.

One way I have tried to clarify a difficult subject is by making a tiny pocket-able book about it. The first one I did was *The Smallest Ever Guide to the Internet (for busy people)* for a meeting of Fortune 500 CEOs, held in Barcelona, Spain. In 1996, many executives knew little about the Internet, while they were overseeing employees who were using it every day. The idea of the meeting was to allow the CEOs a 'safe' place, away from their offices, where they could admit their ignorance and get hands-on training. My job was to tell them how the Internet works. I knew that each attendee would be sitting behind a computer with their own personal technician sitting right next to them, so I doubted that anyone would listen to me. At the start of the lecture, each CEO was handed a copy of the book, *(below, one spread, actual size).*

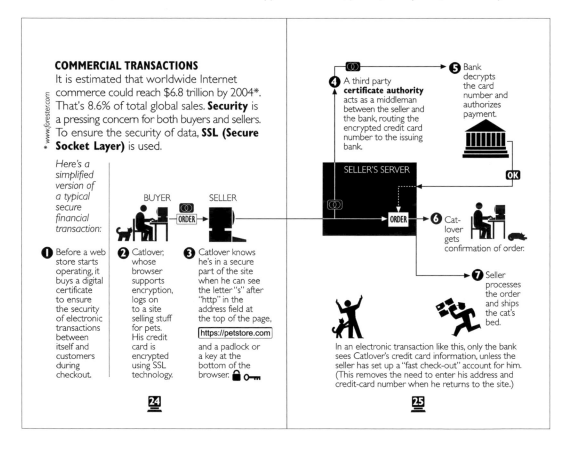

COMMERCIAL TRANSACTIONS
It is estimated that worldwide Internet commerce could reach $6.8 trillion by 2004*. That's 8.6% of total global sales. **Security** is a pressing concern for both buyers and sellers. To ensure the security of data, **SSL (Secure Socket Layer)** is used.

www.forrester.com

Here's a simplified version of a typical secure financial transaction:

BUYER   SELLER   ORDER

❶ Before a web store starts operating, it buys a digital certificate to ensure the security of electronic transactions between itself and customers during checkout.

❷ Catlover, whose browser supports encryption, logs on to a site selling stuff for pets. His credit card is encrypted using SSL technology.

❸ Catlover knows he's in a secure part of the site when he can see the letter "s" after "http" in the address field at the top of the page,

https://petstore.com

and a padlock or a key at the bottom of the browser. 🔒 ⚿

❹ A third party **certificate authority** acts as a middleman between the seller and the bank, routing the encrypted credit card number to the issuing bank.

❺ Bank decrypts the card number and authorizes payment.

SELLER'S SERVER

OK

ORDER

❻ Cat-lover gets confirmation of order.

❼ Seller processes the order and ships the cat's bed.

In an electronic transaction like this, only the bank sees Catlover's credit card information, unless the seller has set up a "fast check-out" account for him. (This removes the need to enter his address and credit-card number when he returns to the site.)

24   25

I didn't have the guts to hold up the book and say *'Everything I'm about to tell you is in here, so I'll shut up and let you get back to your new friend, the computer,'* and then leave the podium.

Nobody listened to the talk. But the little book was very successful, because it was friendly, and jargon-free, and the CEOs took it home with them. And because it was very small, it somehow signaled that even if the subject was difficult, or new, this wasn't going to be difficult to understand. Between the 1996 meeting and 2002, I made seven editions of the Internet book, updating it and printing a total of 15,000 copies.

More *Smallest Guides* followed, *(below)*. Some were just for fun: *Cocktails; Chocolate; Red Hat* (a wordless story about a drummer); *Endangered Animals ABC*. Others were serious: *Life Sciences* for Juan Enriquez of Harvard University; *Billion People Project*, for Della van Heyst; *Investments*, for Phillip Kasofsky and Michael Harvey.

Simplify your color

There was a time when color was expensive to print. Then, when it wasn't, editors and publishers thought everything should be in color: photos, graphics, headlines. Their rationale went like this: One: We're paying for it, so let's use it. Two: The world is in color, why shouldn't your graphics be, too?

For infographics, the comeback answer is simple: color should never be decorative; never used to make a page look better, or more 'informational'. If you use color selectively it is a good way to indicate why a certain part of your graphic is important. Color draws the reader's attention: the accident happened *here*. *This* data point is what you should consider. *This* is the part of your brain that lights up when you are happy. There's plenty of color in editorial photographs and advertisements; simple, restricted color makes infographics stand out when seen in the context of the whole publication.

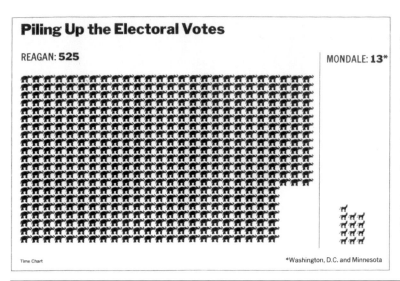

Piling Up the Electoral Votes

REAGAN: **525**

MONDALE: **13***

Time Chart

*Washington, D.C. and Minnesota

There was no color, just black and white, available on the page that this ran on.

In 1984, Time and other media outlets in the US used red for Democrats and blue for Republicans, so these would have been little blue elephants.

Red is still the color of left-leaning political parties in the rest of the world.

If no point in the graphic is more important than any other, black is a fine color all by itself. In November 1984, I saw that there was a tiny elephant and a tiny donkey in the fonts that *Time* used. This was before the art department produced layouts or created graphics with computers. On election night, I asked the typesetter to prepare a stack of the two political parties' symbols, and be ready to assign the final number of electoral votes to each when they were counted. The result was the first chart I made without any drawing or pasting up.

Same size

If you can show something at the size it is in real life, you'll be a long way to making it understandable. This laminated business card, includes a life-size photo of an insect that bores into trees on the front, with other info on the back. The card speaks for itself. It's simplicity in action—that punched exit hole is perfect.

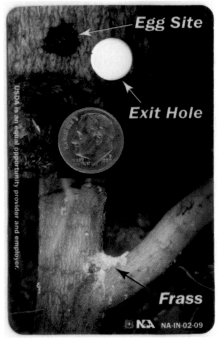

Editing

Editing is a dirty word in some infographic circles. I don't mean that you should angrily shout *EDITING!* when you stub your toe, or when the computer crashes before you've saved some work still in progress. A hearty #@*! is more fulfilling.

The anti-'editing' cohort says that when you edit, you are making a choice about what to present. It's the 'just the facts' argument about impartiality. I believe that most readers *want* an edited version of whatever data is available. They are busy, and they don't necessarily feel the need to interact with the data and come to their own conclusions. The arguers come back: doesn't editing mean that you are selecting just the bits that you want to be seen? NO!! It means that you are trimming off the parts that do not meaningfully contribute to a story.

Besides, all infographics have selections in them of one sort or another: where did the data come from? Do you trust the source? Did you check with two other sources to see any discrepancies? Which parts can be left out without distorting the story, or be seen to be biased? (Or, not only seen, but *be* biased.) Both designers and their readers benefit from the work of editors. Editing clarifies messages.

Labelling

A powerful but underused way to help readers understand your charts and maps and diagrams is to place clear, readable labels directly onto the image, not as numbered captions below it

Right, the back cover of a medical guide to diagostic tests that acted as a contents page.

Who wants to bob their head up and down from a number on the chart or diagram to a caption underneath or beside it? Some labels are just labels: a simple list of what's in the graphic, so put the text next to what needs to be labelled.

Other labels are extra signals to alert the reader to take note of a particular item in the graphic. Look at your chart or diagram as though it's for the first time, and ask: what's the meaning of that unusual outlier—one that's much higher or much lower—in a series of numbers? Or: at

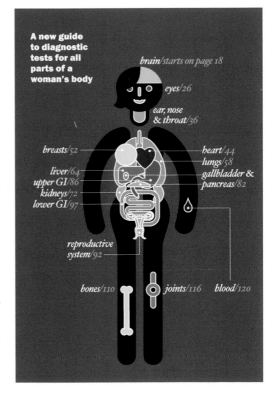

A new guide to diagnostic tests for all parts of a woman's body

brain/starts on page 18
eyes/26
ear, nose & throat/36
breasts/52
heart/44
lungs/58
liver/64
gallbladder & pancreas/82
upper GI/86
kidneys/72
lower GI/97
reproductive system/92
bones/110
joints/116
blood/120

which data point did the story behind the data take a turn for the better, or worse? Or: what was happening in the world to make that spike in numbers? And why? Tell us! Label it! These labels are not part of the dataset, or research you are working with; rather, they are a separate level of information, designed to help. Add a text box with an arrow pointing to where your reader should pay attention. Yes, it's messier, but you are thinking about the person reading your work, not the design of it.

I often try to help readers see the important points by making a kind of 'Greek Chorus' that comments on the action in the chart or diagram. You can do this by drawing tiny people speaking about the graphic right there on the page at the side of the image, *(below)*.

Your little characters may even appear more than once, comic-book style (complete with speech balloons) having a conversation amongst themselves about what's going on in the infographic, explaining parts of it from a different point of view. In effect, they are breaking the 'fourth wall,' by addressing the reader directly, outside the chart itself.

HOW YOU HEAR

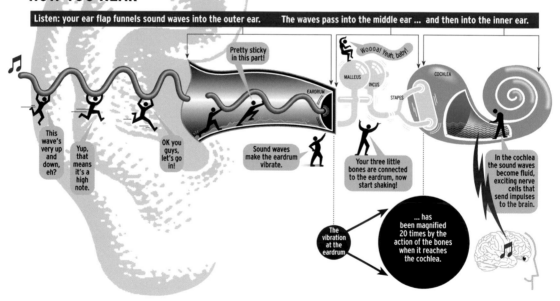

Above, Labels that are a (literal) running commentary on the graphic. From Attaché magazine, 1999. (There's that ear again!)

Another one from Attaché, (right). Here the text here is treated as a series of comic book panels. George Washington's comment at the bottom is even truer now than when it was published in 1998.

HOW A BILL BECOMES LAW

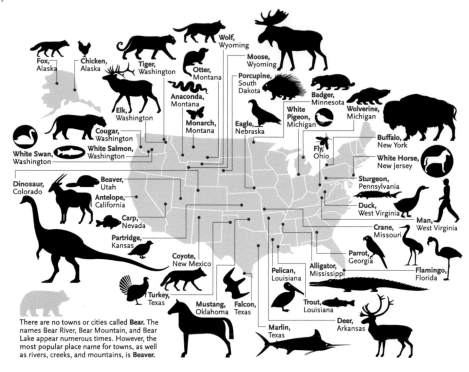

Labels directly attached to their subject. From Navigator Magazine, 2006

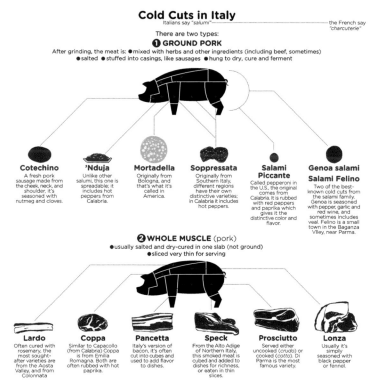

Intro text is minimal; the rest, just labels. From Food and Drink Infographics, 2018

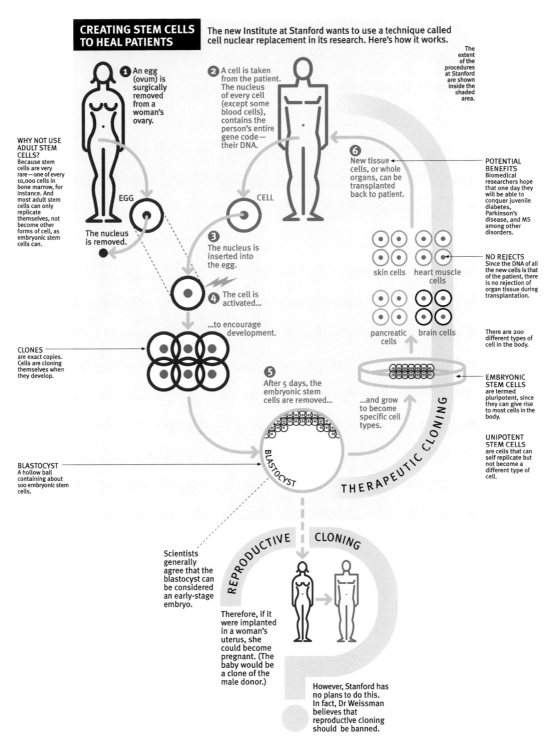

CREATING STEM CELLS TO HEAL PATIENTS

The new Institute at Stanford wants to use a technique called cell nuclear replacement in its research. Here's how it works.

The extent of the procedures at Stanford are shown inside the shaded area.

1 An egg (ovum) is surgically removed from a woman's ovary.

2 A cell is taken from the patient. The nucleus of every cell (except some blood cells), contains the person's entire gene code— their DNA.

WHY NOT USE ADULT STEM CELLS? Because stem cells are very rare—one of every 10,000 cells in bone marrow, for instance. And most adult stem cells can only replicate themselves, not become other forms of cell, as embryonic stem cells can.

EGG

CELL

The nucleus is removed.

3 The nucleus is inserted into the egg.

4 The cell is activated...

...to encourage development.

6 New tissue cells, or whole organs, can be transplanted back to patient.

POTENTIAL BENEFITS Biomedical researchers hope that one day they will be able to conquer juvenile diabetes, Parkinson's disease, and MS among other disorders.

skin cells   heart muscle cells

NO REJECTS Since the DNA of all the new cells is that of the patient, there is no rejection of organ tissue during transplantation.

pancreatic cells   brain cells

There are 200 different types of cell in the body.

CLONES are exact copies. Cells are cloning themselves when they develop.

5 After 5 days, the embryonic stem cells are removed...

...and grow to become specific cell types.

THERAPEUTIC CLONING

EMBRYONIC STEM CELLS are termed pluripotent, since they can give rise to most cells in the body.

UNIPOTENT STEM CELLS are cells that can self replicate but not become a different type of cell.

BLASTOCYST A hollow ball containing about 100 embryonic stem cells.

BLASTOCYST

Scientists generally agree that the blastocyst can be considered an early-stage embryo.

REPRODUCTIVE   CLONING

Therefore, if it were implanted in a woman's uterus, she could become pregnant. (The baby would be a clone of the male donor.)

However, Stanford has no plans to do this. In fact, Dr Weissman believes that reproductive cloning should be banned.

Two levels of info—the main graphic is the tan area. It could have run just like that, but we added explanatory labels in black type around it. This is the version I sent to Bambi Nicklen, art director of Stanford magazine. Dr Weissman, profiled in the related article, fiercely objected to us showing human figures inside the question mark, so we removed them, but left all the text. If I didn't believe it before, I do now: pictures speak louder than words!

HIGH AS A HOUSE

Next time you go to the zoo, amaze your parents with these facts about the tallest animals living there.

Apart from zoos around the world, giraffes are only found in **Africa**. There are between 110,000 to 150,000 of them living there.

These colored areas are where the nine different giraffe patterns are found in Africa.

Funny bumps
Giraffes are born with skin-covered horns (called *ossicones*). Females have tufts of hair on top of their horns, males are bald.

I can see you
The combination of acute eyesight and great height enables giraffes to communicate with each other up to **one mile** away.

Tasty
A 20-inch-long, blue-black tongue covered with sticky saliva enables giraffes to carefully gather acacia leaves, their favorite food, without hurting their mouths on the thorny parts. They eat for 16 to 20 hours a day and consume about **75 pounds** of leaves.

Acacia leaves

What to wear today?
A giraffe's coat comes in **two patterns**: one looks like a net of pale lines on a brown background (called *reticulated*), the other has blotches on a light background, like this one.

There are **nine regional variations** of the two basic patterns. Colors vary from light tan to almost black, and as the animals grow older (they can live for about 25 years in the wild), their colors get darker.

Giraffe patterns are like our fingerprints—none is exactly the same as another.

Stick your neck out
The giraffe's neck has **seven vertebrae**, the same number as a human's.

Drink up
Even though their necks are very long, giraffes' mouths don't reach the ground! They have to kneel to drink water, and need **10 gallons a day**; but most of that comes from the acacia leaves they eat.

Short Zzzzzzzzs
Giraffes usually sleep standing up, with one eye open. But they only take five minute naps (adding up to a **total of 20 minutes** out of every 24 hours). If one falls over onto its side it is very hard to get up, and may die.

Eating is complicated!
Unlike humans, giraffes have **four stomachs.** After chewing leaves and swallowing them, the food is softened in the first stomach and sent back up to the giraffe's mouth where it's chewed a second time. (Cows do this, too; it's called *chewing the cud*.) The cud is swallowed again and passes through the other stomachs where it's completely broken down.

Happy birthday?
When a baby giraffe (called a cub) is born, it weighs **150 pounds** and falls 6 feet to the ground...

...but it's already 6 feet tall. The cub starts walking in one hour, and grows an inch every day. In one year it will reach **12 feet.**

Speedy
With such long legs giraffes can gallop along at **35 mph** for short distances. Each step they take is 15 feet.

Bathtime
Well, actually, giraffes never bathe. Instead they rely on birds (like these yellow-billed oxpeckers) to peck ticks and insects from their skin.

Yuck! When did we last give this guy a "bath"?

Dunno. But look at these juicy insects!

Male giraffes can grow this high.

Zookeepers feed their giraffes special treats like raw onions and carrots. And when it's time to go into the (tall) houses for the night, the keepers often have a hard time persuading the animals to obey their orders; giraffes have minds of their own!

18 feet
16 feet
14 feet
12 feet
10 feet
8 feet
6 feet
4 feet
2 feet

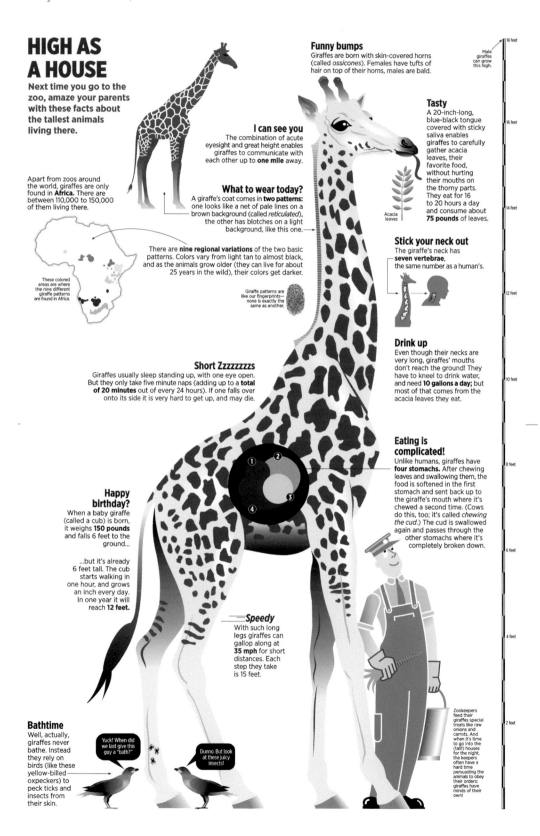

For the giraffe graphic (left), aimed at children, the text is split up into a series of labels. As with many of my pieces, there's some commentary at the bottom, but this time it's factual, not there just for fun!

Phew! This is a long chapter!

And 'labelling' is only number 7.

Humans must like the sound of their own sentences.

I like Negronis.

Drawing

I was trained as an illustrator, and still love the physical act of drawing. There's something about the direct contact of pencil or pen with paper that excites me. That path from eye-to-brain-to-hand-to-paper is not the same as mouse-to-screen. It's possible that new generations of i-Pads with digital pencils may change my mind.

In art school I drew from live models and 'still' life arrangements of fruit or classical busts. Now I draw almost every day in the summer at a nearby beach; often in the white spaces in newspaper advertisements. Sometimes there's a nice sky at the top of the ad; I stick that onto some simple foreground drawing. Pure white drawing paper is scary; newsprint is forgiving, and just right for a fast sketch. It's the act of looking that matters, not the art materials.

Compo Beach May 17/2017

Looking—looking hard—at your subject, and drawing it, whatever it is—a picnic table, or a small boat in the middle distance—is good practice for making better graphics. Don't think of drawing as something that captures surface likenesses, with light and shadow and all those arty connotations. The great designer and artist Milton Glaser once said that the difference between illustration and drawing is this: *illustration* is about surface appearances; *drawing* is about drawing out—extracting—the meaning of the subject. (Not that there's a great deal of meaning in a picnic table, but I get the point, Milton, and thank you.)

Thinking about drawing and the role of traditionally constructed perspective can help you make sure that readers understand your graphic. Here's a simple demonstration about how we perceive things, and the part perspective plays in affecting what we see *(opposite)*.

BIGGER BOATS, OR JUST BIGGER BECAUSE THEY ARE CLOSER?

1. *For a chart about the relative lengths of warships, the data provided was a simple bar chart.*

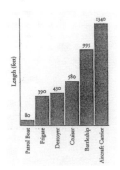

2. *Since ships are horizontal, not vertical, it was natural to rotate the chart. (But now the patrol boat appears to be taller than it is long!)*

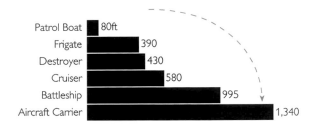

3. *In place of the bars, I drew silhouettes of the ships to scale.*

4. *Is this picture OK?*

   NO, because what you see here looks like a scene of docked boats, naturally receding into the distance.

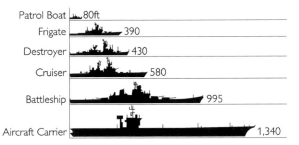

5. *Placing the ships from smallest at the top to largest at the bottom might be logical, but perspective makes it appear as if they are smaller at the top because they are further away from you, not because they are smaller. Perspective overrides any other visual interpretation.*

6. *Simple answer: reverse the order of the ships. This flattens the chart, and removes the perspective effect.*

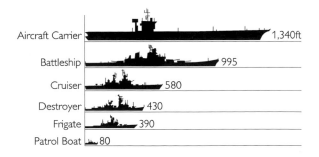

The marriage of 'real' drawing with hard-edged, computer-generated artwork is an interesting way to make reader-friendly infographics. David Driver, the Art Director of the *Radio Times,* realized that by combining the talents of two of his regular contributors he could have, in effect, a third conributor. He offered me many jobs that benefitted enormously from this kind of collaboration with illustrators. On the following pages are three examples.

Peter Brookes is now the celebrated cartoonist at *The Times,* in London. He was one of the artists that David paired me with. We collaborated on several 'Behind the Scenes' graphics—these were technical and other aspects of how current events were broadcast by the BBC.

I asked Peter for his memories of our joint efforts celebrating the 1975 Apollo/Soyuz mission. (*See next spread.*)

'I enjoyed very much the experience of working alongside someone else with a quite separate set of professional disciplines to my own (though in reality mine was much the lesser role). There was a heightened sense of creativity putting together spreads of 'infographics' for Radio Times where ideas could be bounced off each other. Marrying our different styles was exciting and, for me, new.

This (Apollo/Soyuz link-up) *was the piece which I think resonated most with me of all our 'Behind the Scenes' work. As a project it had everything: a first in space (the joint Apollo/Soyuz mission involving a historic handshake between Stafford and Leonov, the US and Soviet commanders); a great opportunity to marry our styles in one mega-graphic; the chance to incorporate interview quotes with the astronauts, and to extend the whole thing with a cover illustration drawn by Nigel (right) and two black and white programme page graphics, (one of them, opposite).*

'I loved incorporating portraits of these heroic participants in our tribute to such an inspiring event. (By the way, they were glory days which could never happen now....imagine Putin and Biden thinking it was a good idea!). The difficulty of combining a mono newsprint page with a full-colour page to make a spread was overcome by placing the docked pair of spacecraft right across it. It couldn't have worked better in my opinion. In fact it was more than exciting to work on...it was out of this world!'

OK, Peter, don't get carried away…but I have to agree, it *was* exciting!

One of the great things about the *Radio Times* projects was that David always treated us as more than artists; he made sure that people were available so that we could gather the necessary information, and in the case of the astronauts, he allowed us to interview them ourselves. We set up a slightly amateur phone-plus-extension-phone system—elaborate for the time!—in my house in London to conduct the interviews. As Peter says: '*Without David's organising genius and enthusiasm, we'd have been far less effective.*'

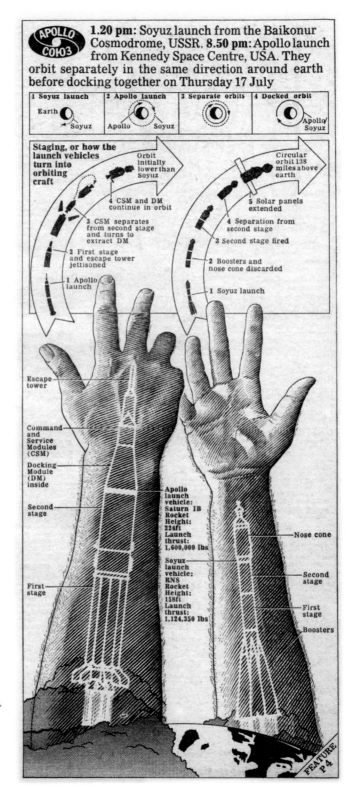

1.20 pm: Soyuz launch from the Baikonur Cosmodrome, USSR. **8.50 pm:** Apollo launch from Kennedy Space Centre, USA. They orbit separately in the same direction around earth before docking together on Thursday 17 July

1 Soyuz launch	2 Apollo launch	3 Separate orbits	4 Docked orbit
Earth	Apollo Soyuz		Apollo/ Soyuz
Soyuz			

Staging, or how the launch vehicles turn into orbiting craft

Orbit initially lower than Soyuz

Circular orbit 138 miles above earth

4 CSM and DM continue in orbit

3 CSM separates from second stage and turns to extract DM

2 First stage and escape tower jettisoned

1 Apollo launch

5 Solar panels extended

4 Separation from second stage

3 Second stage fired

2 Boosters and nose cone discarded

1 Soyuz launch

Escape tower

Command and Service Modules (CSM)

Docking Module (DM) inside

Second stage

First stage

Apollo launch vehicle: Saturn IB Rocket Height: 224ft Launch thrust: 1,600,000 lbs

Soyuz launch vehicle: RNS Rocket Height: 158ft Launch thrust: 1,124,350 lbs

Nose cone

Second stage

First stage

Boosters

FEATURE P4

Among his other styles, Peter had a way of drawing that mimicked old black and white engravings. Apart from looking good, they reproduced really well on the rough newsprint pages of Radio Times, and gave our joint work an authority and humanity I could never have achieved if I had done this part of the art myself. I stepped back and did minimal graphics on top of the outstretched arms, which continued the theme of the handshake in space.

Next spread, another of Peter's styles: fully rendered portraits.

At 1.20 BST on Tuesday, a Soyuz spacecraft will lift off from the Baikonur launch complex in the USSR. About seven-and-a-half hours later, an Apollo spacecraft will be launched from the Kennedy Space Centre in the USA. After 44 hours they will dock together in space. The first international space link-up is previewed here by **Peter Brookes** and **Nigel Holmes**, who spoke to the American astronauts for RADIO TIMES

The big handshake

Apollo/Soyuz from Tuesday BBC1 Colour, Radio 2

'IT IS A new technology; with a view to future rendezvous, and rescue. A whole basis for mutual co-operation,' says Apollo Commander Thomas Stafford, the first man to transfer from one nation's spacecraft into another's during this week's Apollo/Soyuz Test Project (ASTP).

On 24 May 1972, the United States and the Soviet Union agreed on the organisation of a joint test docking mission in earth orbit. The three American astronauts and two Russian cosmonauts, pictured here, will test the docking system developed over the last three years, using it to exchange visits between the Apollo and Soyuz craft where they will conduct joint scientific experiments.

The whole mission will last nine days – from Soyuz lift-off on Tuesday to Apollo splashdown in the Pacific at 22.19 BST on 24 July, three-and-a-half days after Soyuz has landed in Russia. The two craft stay in the docked position for two days.

And what will they exchange? Soyuz pilot Alexei Leonov: ' We shall turn over a casket of about 1,500 seeds of the best varieties of our apples to the Apollo crew, and will receive the same kind of present from them. In addition, on board there will be halves of souvenir medals. Each crew will have the missing half and will join them to form a unique medal.'

And for us earth-bound viewers, the pictures from space should be better than from previous missions. For the first time a communications satellite will be used to relay live and recorded colour television pictures from the orbiting craft.●

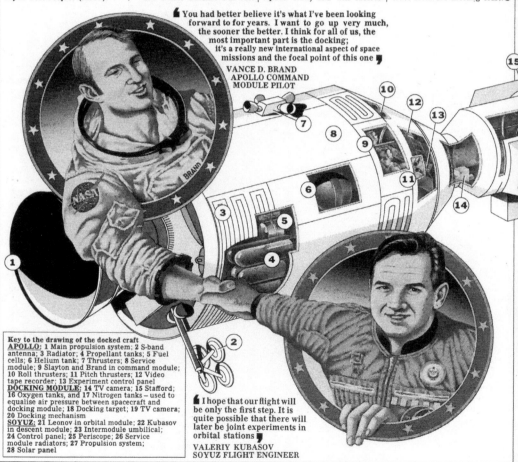

"You had better believe it's what I've been looking forward to for years. I want to go up very much, the sooner the better. I think for all of us, the most important part is the docking; it's a really new international aspect of space missions and the focal point of this one"

VANCE D. BRAND
APOLLO COMMAND
MODULE PILOT

Key to the drawing of the docked craft
APOLLO: 1 Main propulsion system; 2 S-band antenna; 3 Radiator; 4 Propellant tanks; 5 Fuel cells; 6 Helium tank; 7 Thrusters; 8 Service module; 9 Slayton and Brand in command module; 10 Roll thrusters; 11 Pitch thrusters; 12 Video tape recorder; 13 Experiment control panel **DOCKING MODULE:** 14 TV camera; 15 Stafford; 16 Oxygen tanks, and 17 Nitrogen tanks – used to equalise air pressure between spacecraft and docking module; 18 Docking target; 19 TV camera; 20 Docking mechanism
SOYUZ: 21 Leonov in orbital module; 22 Kubasov in descent module; 23 Intermodule umbilical; 24 Control panel; 25 Periscope; 26 Service module radiators; 27 Propulsion system; 28 Solar panel

"I hope that our flight will be only the first step. It is quite possible that there will later be joint experiments in orbital stations"

VALERIY KUBASOV
SOYUZ FLIGHT ENGINEER

Astronaut portraits by Peter Brookes, capsules and docking station by me. Art Director David Driver

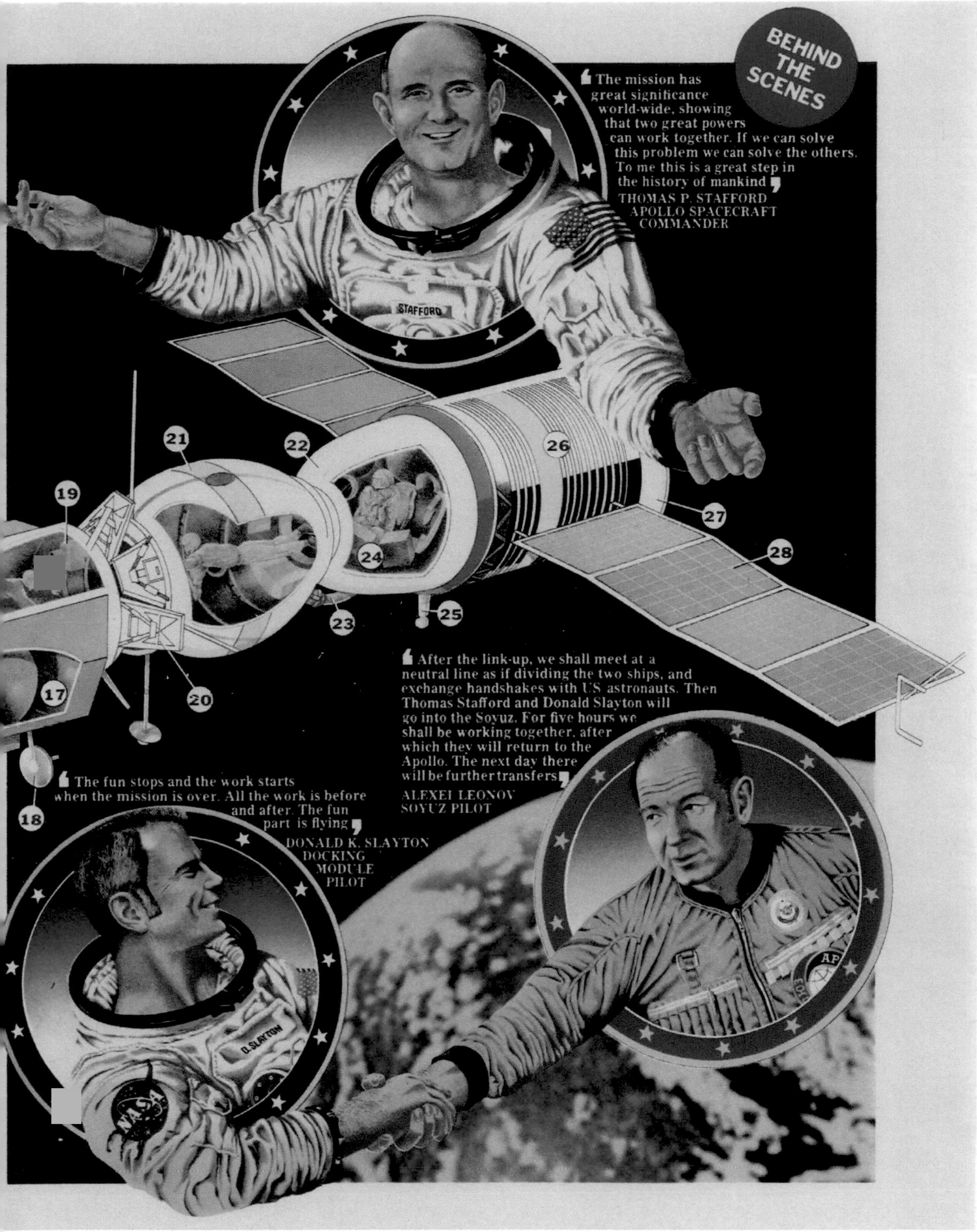

BEHIND THE SCENES

❝The mission has great significance world-wide, showing that two great powers can work together. If we can solve this problem we can solve the others. To me this is a great step in the history of mankind❞
THOMAS P. STAFFORD
APOLLO SPACECRAFT COMMANDER

21

22

26

19

24

27

28

23

25

17

20

❝After the link-up, we shall meet at a neutral line as if dividing the two ships, and exchange handshakes with US astronauts. Then Thomas Stafford and Donald Slayton will go into the Soyuz. For five hours we shall be working together, after which they will return to the Apollo. The next day there will be further transfers❞
ALEXEI LEONOV
SOYUZ PILOT

❝The fun stops and the work starts when the mission is over. All the work is before and after. The fun part is flying❞
DONALD K. SLAYTON
DOCKING MODULE PILOT

18

In 1975, when this spread was published, the Radio Times magazine sent color pages to the printer several days in advance of the black and white ones. Also, the color pages were printed on smooth, coated paper, while the rest was newsprint. Somehow, it always worked!

Another 'Behind the Scenes' graphic I did with Peter was about how the radio and TV announcer Frank Bough juggled his live commentary from two different sports, *(below)*.

Peter on this one:

'It helped that my own style as an illustrator was somewhat 'straight-forward' and not too idiosyncratic. This might have got in the way of our narrative, which had to be direct and to the point. In this exercise of delivering information in a combination of words and pictures, it could all have gone horribly wrong! But I do believe we cracked it, and it was enormously satisfying to work on.'

Peter continued:

'Another aspect which particularly interested me in our joint work, and which spilled over into my separate work as an illustrator (and still does now that I'm a political cartoonist) is the need to refine and edit continually in order to make things immediately comprehensible to the reader. Less is more. Of course, there should be enough content to make the whole thing interesting, but the message must be CLEAR. We were taking up whole spreads in Radio Times and I currently occupy half a page a day on The Times, so readers have to have their money's worth!

'Ideas, and the use of wit or humour in graphic work can have their difficulties. One person's comprehension of the artist's intention is not another's, but you have to try to keep this mismatch to a minimum. All I ever try to do is to engage as many people as I can, and as directly as I can.'

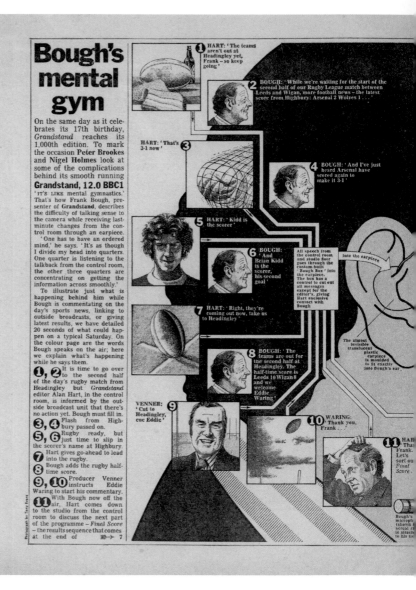

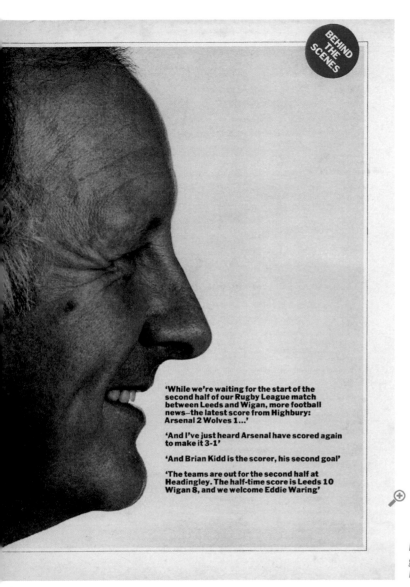

BEHIND THE SCENES

'While we're waiting for the start of the second half of our Rugby League match between Leeds and Wigan, more football news—the latest score from Highbury: Arsenal 2 Wolves 1...'

'And I've just heard Arsenal have scored again to make it 3-1'

'And Brian Kidd is the scorer, his second goal'

'The teams are out for the second half at Headingley. The half-time score is Leeds 10 Wigan 8, and we welcome Eddie Waring'

Left page: people by Peter; graphic arrangement by me. Right page: photo by Tony Evans

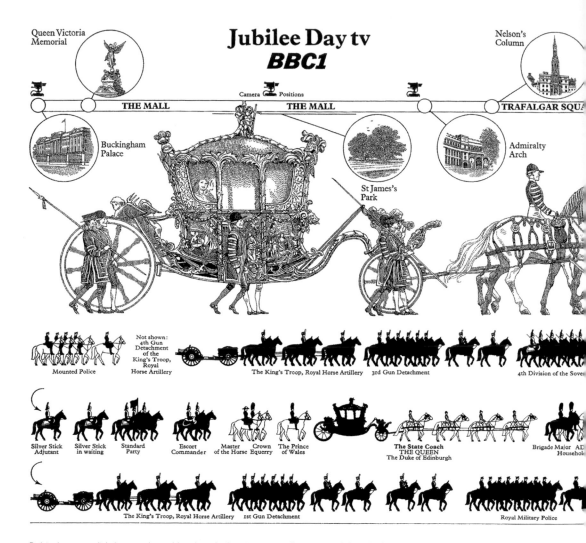

Robin Jacques did the coach and landmark drawings; my silhouettes of the whole procession are underneath.

David was so good at planning, that in a joint effort with another artist, Robin Jacques, we never met face-to-face while we worked separately on Queen Elizabeth's Silver Jubilee Procession from Buckingham Palace to St. Paul's Cathedral, *(above)*. That's what good art directors do: they set you up with how much space you have, put you in touch with a collaborator, then leave you alone to decide how to proceed. Robin's beautifully executed drawing of the Royal Coach coupled with my simple graphic silhouettes show the best of our individual styles, and readers get a fuller picture of the splendor, *and* the details, of the event.

While I was writing this, the Queen was celebrating her Platinum Jubilee, marking 70 years on the throne, and people all over the United Kingdom were having picnic teas. Queen Elizabeth died on September 8th, 2022. Long live King Charles III.

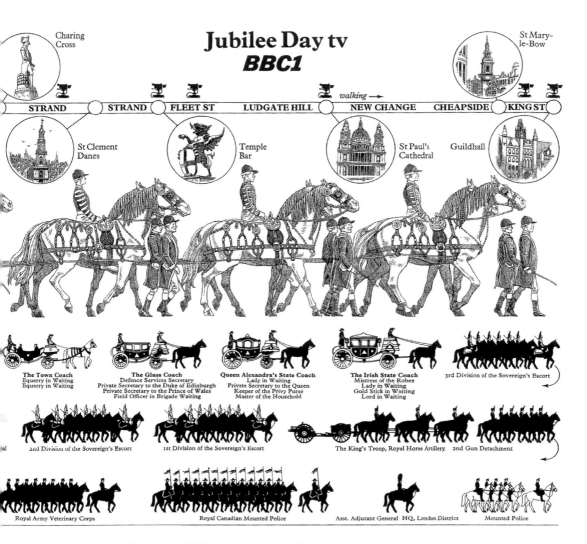

From the Radio Times, June 1977. Art Director David Driver

My realistic little sihouettes here are one way to draw, but early in my career I realized that drawing people as elements *in charts* wasn't that different from drawing abstract bars to represent people. Also it let the reader know that the chart was *about* people. It's funny when people marvel at an ability to draw, telling you they can't even draw a straight line. The easy riposte is that no one can—we use a ruler! (And lots of other 'cheating' tools to make perfect circles and ovals.)

I believe that anyone can draw; most of us naturally did so as unselfconscious children. We made stickmen and women with straight lines and round heads. I made a half-joking handout showing what I meant for a conference that consisted mostly of writers and editors. *(See the next page.)*

Art for editors—how to draw stuff All you need are a few boxes, lines, and circles.

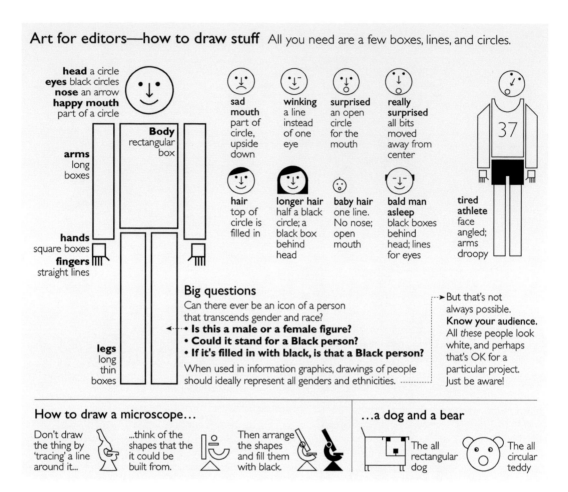

head a circle
eyes black circles
nose an arrow
happy mouth
part of a circle

Body
rectangular
box

arms
long
boxes

hands
square boxes
fingers
straight lines

legs
long
thin
boxes

**sad
mouth**
part of
circle,
upside
down

winking
a line
instead
of one
eye

surprised
an open
circle
for the
mouth

**really
surprised**
all bits
moved
away from
center

hair
top of
circle is
filled in

longer hair
half a black
circle; a
black box
behind
head

baby hair
one line.
No nose;
open
mouth

**bald man
asleep**
black boxes
behind
head; lines
for eyes

**tired
athlete**
face
angled;
arms
droopy

37

Big questions
Can there ever be an icon of a person
that transcends gender and race?
• **Is this a male or a female figure?**
• **Could it stand for a Black person?**
• **If it's filled in with black, is that a Black person?**
When used in information graphics, drawings of people
should ideally represent all genders and ethnicities.

But that's not
always possible.
Know your audience.
All *these* people look
white, and perhaps
that's OK for a
particular project.
Just be aware!

How to draw a microscope...
Don't draw
the thing by
'tracing' a line
around it...

...think of the
shapes that the
it could be
built from.

Then arrange
the shapes
and fill them
with black.

...a dog and a bear
The all
rectangular
dog

The all
circular
teddy

At the start of my freelance career, I never completely believed in my drawing ability, so I *did* rely on rulers, compasses, t-squares, lots of oval and circle templates, and ship's curves, to produce smooth, clean lines, drawn with always-clogging-up *Rapidograph* pens. (Ship's curves are 18-inch long pieces of stiff clear plastic, used like rulers to produce swooping lines that range from almost straight to long, gentle arcs; the kind of thing great uncle George would have used to draw ships.) This was before I got a computer, and drawing with these mechanical aids meant that when I did get a Mac, the transfer to a completely mechanical method of drawing was easier for me than it was for illustrators who drew more freely, but felt they had to change and use a computer. (They didn't.) I'm amused that the drawing program I started with was called *Freehand,* since using a computer to draw is the opposite of free drawing.

But lately, some 35 years into using a computer, I have incorporated occasional, actual freehand drawing which, when scanned, adds a human touch to the work, *(right and following page).*

*The workings of a saxophone from Attaché magazine, 1999.
The grayed-down drawing carries the whole thing, while
minimal infographic marks do the explaining.*

HOW THE SAXOPHONE WORKS

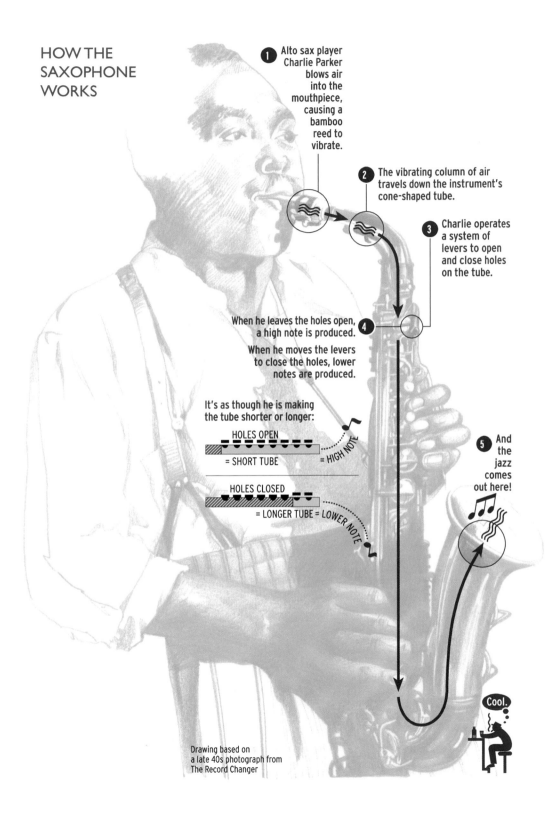

1 Alto sax player Charlie Parker blows air into the mouthpiece, causing a bamboo reed to vibrate.

2 The vibrating column of air travels down the instrument's cone-shaped tube.

3 Charlie operates a system of levers to open and close holes on the tube.

4 When he leaves the holes open, a high note is produced.

When he moves the levers to close the holes, lower notes are produced.

It's as though he is making the tube shorter or longer:

HOLES OPEN

= SHORT TUBE   = HIGH NOTE

HOLES CLOSED

= LONGER TUBE = LOWER NOTE

5 And the jazz comes out here!

Cool.

Drawing based on a late 40s photograph from The Record Changer

Naadam

The three games are an Eastern version of the ancient Olympics. Originally just for men, **women now take part in archery and horse racing.** Celebrations and sports events are held in many parts of the country, but the largest, the **National Naadam,** is held in the National Sports Stadium in Ulaanbaatar, the country's capital. After an **opening ceremony** with dancers, musicians, athletes, and riders, the games begin:

1 MONGOLIAN TRADITIONAL WRESTLING matches have **no time limit, and no size classification:** the wrestler with the greatest fame has the privilege of picking his opponent. There are nine or ten rounds (depending on the total number of wrestlers).

Each wrestler has a designated *zasuul* who sings songs of praise to the winner.

Wrestlers must wear traditional tight shoulder vests, and very short shorts.

A wrestler loses when any part of his body, other than hands and feet, touches the ground.

Left, detail of a graphic from my book Crazy Competitions that includes scanned drawings. The energy of the wrestlers is better represented by 'real' drawing.

Watching a polo match

The horses are called "ponies", and it costs an arm and a leg to own them, train them and transport them, so it might not be a sport you'll ever play yourself. But it is exciting to watch. And you get to go onto the field at half-time!

The mallet, or polo stick, is made of manau cane. Its length is tailored to each player.

The ball is hit with the side of the mallet's cigar-shaped head (not with the ends like croquet).

Polo is always played right-handed. The left hand holds the reins.

Most players wear face guards.

Kneepads are essential protection due to close contact with opponents.

Each player owns at least two (but more likely three or four) ponies.

A polo pony is trained to break into a canter from a standing position, and can stop and turn in an instant, responding to subtle leg and hand movements from its rider.

US$100,000 Good ponies are expensive.

Legs are protected by bandages or strap-on boots.

My mum had a riding school, so I grew up riding, and I've always loved drawing horses, but they look stiff if I construct the art with a computer drawing program. On the right is a detail from a piece about what to look out for during a polo match, from The Bigger Book of Everything— a book of graphics that explained how to do (almost!) everything.

 **Adding Humans**

My colleague John Grimwade always urges infographic designers to show some evidence of human presence in their work. Here he is, describing what he calls deadworld:

'Exhibit 1: A fabulous cutaway rendering of a shopping mall in hyper-real 3D. But there's not a person to be seen. First and foremost, the addition of just one person would immediately add an effective sense of scale. Then there's the eerie post-apocalyptic effect of busy spaces with no one in them. When I look at this kind of infographic, I'm thinking that it's 3am and someone has left the lights on.

'Of course, it's not necessary to add a realistic number of people. It's more important that the graphic is clear and explanatory. But infographics with no sign of human life have always seemed strange to me. And cold.'

I've included people in many charts, not just those where an actual human would, as John says, add a sense of scale. The reason is the same as his: a person, of any kind, in a chart gives the reader something to identify with.

Empathy and inclusion

Many people, including software developer and writer Jacob Harris (*Connecting with the Dots*), and Texas Tech professor Sam Dragga with author Dan Voss (*Cruel Pies: The Inhumanity of Technical Illustrations*) have written about how images can humanize infographics. In 2015, Harris, a self-described data scold, asked this question about empathetic design:

'Should we even try with our graphics to make readers care? The Devil's Advocate would argue that it's not the responsibility of our interactives to make people feel something about a topic—that is usually handled by a narrative piece paired with them—but I feel that in these days where charts may be tweeted, reblogged, and aggregated out of context, you must assume your graphic will stand alone.'

I agree, and I think joyful infographics should try to make people care by 'seeing' themselves represented in printed or interactive pieces. Also, it's important to remember that busy policymakers may be among those who see your graphic 'standing alone,' so that the way you address empathy can affect the way they see the data about which they will make decisions.

To make their point, Dragga and Voss suggest that Charles-Joseph Minard's well-known chart-map of Napoleon's march could be humanized by adding pictorial icons to show the extent of the deaths in more human terms. They say: *'True, the pictographs are statistically redundant with the diminishing width of the line—but they are not emotionally redundant. In fact, they add the vital element that was missing—the human beings who constitute the fatality figures.'*

While I think the principle is correct here, the result—with icons piled on top of Minard's graphic—is not aesthetically successful. I'm sure that if Minard had wanted to include icons of infantry and grave markers, he would have designed the whole thing differently; but the point is made.

The idea of making charts with little symbols of people has been around for a long time; if we can call Egyptian wall-paintings with lined-up figures 'charts,' then that's a possible starting point. Closer to today, Willard Brinton shows good and bad examples in his 1914 book *Graphic Methods for Presenting Facts*. In the 1920s, Otto Neurath built on that, with his *Isotype* system. In 2014, Alberto Cairo and *ProPublica*'s Scott Klein developed *Wee People*, a font of human silhouettes, drawn by Alberto from photos of the *ProPublica* newsroom staff, that can be lined up to form charts in place of impersonal dots or bars, *(below)*.

There's a question about empathy when the key to a chart states that one of these little people stands in for many. Is it really empathetic for your chart to say one person = 10,000? Unit charts about non-human commodities—cotton, cars or cocoa beans—are fine if you substitute one for many, but charts about people are best when it's one-on-one; when the numbers involved are represented by the same number of icons. It's not always possible to do this, but it should be kept in mind, because when one icon of a person represents many people, the chart is almost as impersonal as when the person is just a dot.

Crossing the street; rating entertainment

You don't mess with some signs: red for stop and green for go. It's instant communication for motorists. But for pedestrians? Let's have some fun, *(below)*. Why be content with generic illuminated stickmen signaling to walkers when they must wait at the curb and when to cross the street? Some cities, especially in Germany, are playing with amusing variations. Karl Marx was born in Trier; Elvis Presley was stationed in Friedberg while he was in the US army in the 1950s. A human approach makes the mundane more enjoyable.

The *Little Man* icons in the *San Francisco Chronicle*'s arts and entertainment reviews use the same human approach. Most entertainment rating systems in magazines or newspapers use stars; thumbs up or down; A+, A, A-, B+, B, etc., or just numbers to grade cinema and musical events. In 1942, Executive Editor Scott Newhall and artist Warren Goodrich introduced the *Chronicle*'s theater and film ratings *Little Man*, *(below)*. He snoozed if he thought a production had problems, he jumped out of his seat with wild applause if he thought it was a 'don't miss' event. His worst review was an empty chair: he had left the building, and you shouldn't bother to go. At 80 years old, he's still as popular as ever.

The *Chronicle*'s website, *SFGate.com,* asked me for some comments about the *Little Man* for an article by Robert Hurwitt about the paper's famous graphic critic. Here's what I said:

'In the late 30s, Fortune magazine and others in the US started to populate their statistical charts with pictorial symbols of people (to represent a number of workers, for example) instead of making charts out of abstract bars or lines. This trend was itself an offshoot of the work of Otto Neurath who pioneered the idea in Europe in the 20s.

When the Little Man first appeared in 1942, the Chronicle was expanding the idea of substituting a human for an abstract symbol (such as a star). And what an inspired expansion it was!

Is the Little Man effective? An emphatic Yes! Because he brings a human element to reviews and so much more information than the usual one- to four- or five-star rating. (Agreeing with his opinion is something else, but that's true of all reviews.)

Should he be updated to reflect today's politically correct ways? I don't think so (although I wouldn't mind trying). Let's accept that not every movie goer is a bald, middle-aged man; that few people wear hats, and that standing on the seats is probably not good for the person sitting next to you. Perhaps we can just be happy that someone at the paper had some fun all those years ago, and that the Little Man has been with us ever since.'

And here's the *Chronicle*'s pop music critic Aidin Vaziri, from the same article:

'Say what you will of the Little Man, but on the rare occasion that he is effectively deployed, it's like putting 16 exclamation marks at the end of a review. The visual rating is way better than a handful of ambiguous stars.'

Personal logos—monograms with a picture

Inspired by the 1920s trademarks of German graphic designers Karl Prinz, Philipp Seitz, Konrad Jochheim, and my favorite, Karl Shulpig, I made pictorial logos for friends' business cards, *(below).* They were a kind of monogram with pictures that attempted to portray both business attributes and, whenever I could, a simplified physical resemblance. (Hair seemed to play a big role.) They lightened up the business of exchanging business cards, and helped remind potential clients of the services offered. And if they made people smile, all the better.

Tommy Meehan
Tile contractor

Erin McKenna
Tilesetter
My wife!

John Hurley
Rock Musician

Neven Telak
Draftsman

Jim Keyser
Carpenter

Nigel Holmes
Chartmaker

Did they last as long as the *Apple* apple, or the *Nike* swoosh? No. But they were fun.

Next pages: examples of graphics where humans have muscled in.

Above, an almost wordless explanation of how Wildfire (a robot, phone-based, personal secretary) works. It seemed right to do a little comic book sequence to explain it. While the robot is exactly the same each time she appears, the humans are in various states of excitement. The text of the article filled the big empty space, but it looks good blank! Esquire magazine, Art Director Robert Priest.

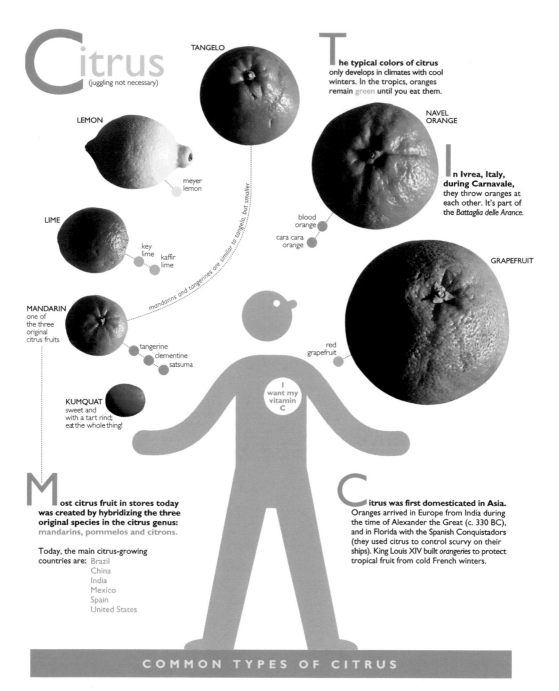

Citrus
(juggling not necessary)

TANGELO

LEMON
meyer lemon

LIME
key lime   kaffir lime

The typical colors of citrus only develops in climates with cool winters. In the tropics, oranges remain green until you eat them.

NAVEL ORANGE

In Ivrea, Italy, during Carnavale, they throw oranges at each other. It's part of the *Battaglia delle Arance*.

blood orange
cara cara orange

mandarins and tangerines are similar to tangelo, but smaller

GRAPEFRUIT

MANDARIN
one of the three original citrus fruits

tangerine
clementine
satsuma

red grapefruit

KUMQUAT
sweet and with a tart rind; eat the whole thing!

I want my vitamin C

Most citrus fruit in stores today was created by hybridizing the three original species in the citrus genus: mandarins, pommelos and citrons.

Today, the main citrus-growing countries are: Brazil
China
India
Mexico
Spain
United States

Citrus was first domesticated in Asia. Oranges arrived in Europe from India during the time of Alexander the Great (c. 330 BC), and in Florida with the Spanish Conquistadors (they used citrus to control scurvy on their ships). King Louis XIV built *orangeries* to protect tropical fruit from cold French winters.

COMMON TYPES OF CITRUS

For Taschen's huge Food Infographics book, I thought photos of citrus fruit would do a better job than anything I could draw. ⊕

UNCLE CENSUS

☐ WHITE ■ HISPANIC ■ BLACK ▨ ASIAN ▨ OTHER

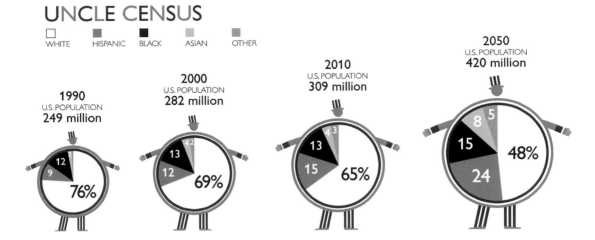

1990
U.S. POPULATION
249 million

12
9
76%

2000
U.S. POPULATION
282 million

13
12
4 2
69%

2010
U.S. POPULATION
309 million

13
15
4 3
65%

2050
U.S. POPULATION
420 million

8 5
15
24
48%

*Serious infographic folks argue about the value
of pie charts, but they sure are fun to play with.*

*Parenting magazine wanted friendly infographics
to help their (mostly female) readers see what
was on the minds of their menfolk.*

Percentage of men who said they'd be better fathers if ...

... their wives didn't work

10%
of all fathers

... they had more money

33%
of all fathers

49%
of single
fathers
under
45

... if they didn't have to work

4%
of those earning
under $25,000

19%
of those earning
$40,000+

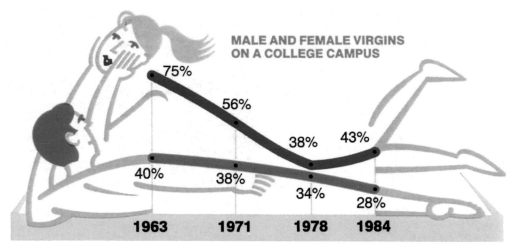

MALE AND FEMALE VIRGINS ON A COLLEGE CAMPUS

75%

56%

38%   43%

40%   38%

34%

28%

1963   1971   1978   1984

This is the kind of chart that academics really hated. It appeared in Glamour magazine, so few of them saw it! But the shape of the lines really contributed to the message of the graph: it was fortuitous that they converged so nicely.

The 'Snapshot' graphics on the front of each section of USA Today came in for a lot of criticism (if not derision) when the paper launched in 1982. Art Director Richard Curtis was aware that his stable of artists were looking a bit too closely at my Time graphics, and he graciously invited me to talk to his team. This barely disguised self-portrait from Time in 1985 included a nod to the real innovation there: George Rorick's groundbreaking back page weather map.

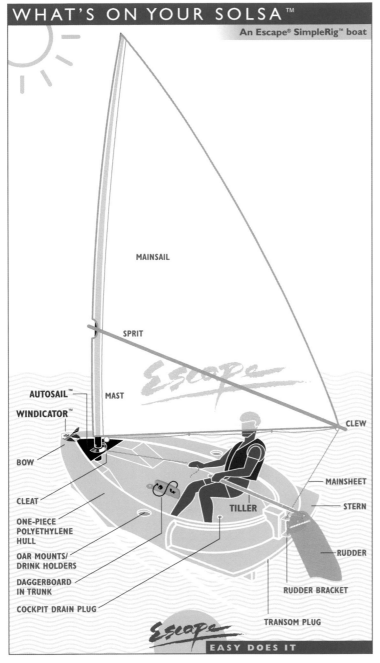

WHAT'S ON YOUR SOLSA™
An Escape® SimpleRig™ boat

MAINSAIL

SPRIT

AUTOSAIL™

WINDICATOR™

MAST

CLEW

BOW

CLEAT

ONE-PIECE
POLYETHYLENE
HULL

OAR MOUNTS/
DRINK HOLDERS

DAGGERBOARD
IN TRUNK

COCKPIT DRAIN PLUG

MAINSHEET

STERN

TILLER

RUDDER

RUDDER BRACKET

TRANSOM PLUG

EASY DOES IT

CAUTION

Safety warning
Sailing can be dangerous and physically demanding. The user of this product understands that sailing may result in serious injury or death. Observe these safety standards:

► Avoid contact between the mast and overhead electrical wires.
► Wear a nationally approved personal flotation device.
► Know how to swim.
► Obtain certified first aid training, and carry first aid and rescue/safety equipment.
► Get an updated local marine weather forecast prior to departure.
► Be aware of harmful weather changes while sailing.
► Share your sailing plans with an attentive friend before departing.
► Dress appropriately for the weather conditions. Cold water and/or weather can result in hypothermia.
► Bring fresh water and drink to avoid dehydration.
► Take precautions to avoid eye and skin damage from exposure to the sun.
► Check your equipment prior to each use for signs of wear or failure.
► Always sail with others in sight.
► Be aware of dangerous currents or tides.
► Avoid breaking waves and/or surf conditions.
► Be aware of other boats.
► Do not exceed your sailing ability.
► Be aware of your limitations.
► Consult your physician prior to your first sail.
► Do not use alcohol or mind-altering drugs prior to or while using this product.
► Never abandon the boat.

RIGHTING THE BOAT

Because of the Escape's exceptional stability, you are very unlikely to capsize. But if you do, getting the boat back upright is no big deal. Here's the sequence:

Adding human figures to graphics is sometimes obvious. Escape Sailboats needed waterproof set-up and sailing instructions for its line of small, bright yellow polyethylene boats. The human figure gives size, context, and life.

At Time magazine I incorporated human figures whenever I could in an effort to bring facts straight into people's lives.

Right, disposable income. Below, what it felt like for a family living in America at the end of the 70s.

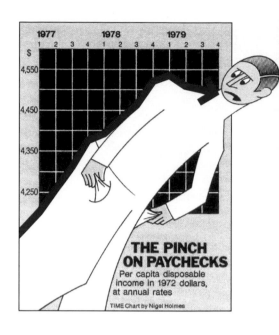

THE PINCH ON PAYCHECKS

Per capita disposable income in 1972 dollars, at annual rates

TIME Chart by Nigel Holmes

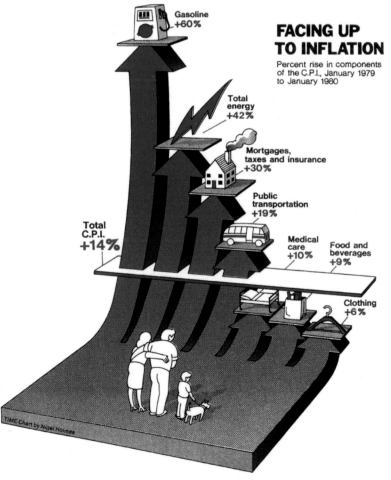

FACING UP TO INFLATION

Percent rise in components of the C.P.I., January 1979 to January 1980

Gasoline +60%

Total energy +42%

Mortgages, taxes and insurance +30%

Public transportation +19%

Medical care +10%

Food and beverages +9%

Total C.P.I. +14%

Clothing +6%

TIME Chart by Nigel Holmes

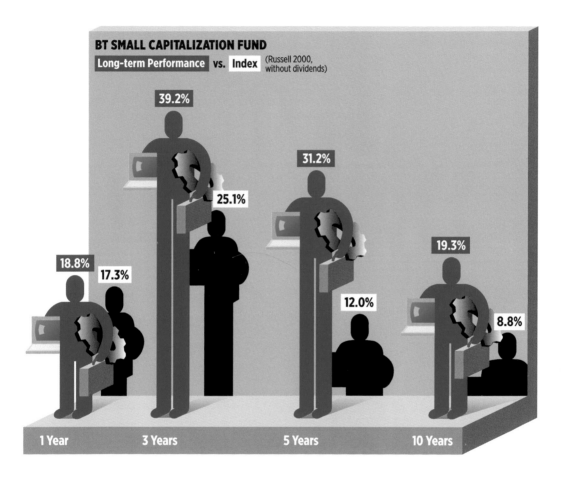

BT SMALL CAPITALIZATION FUND
Long-term Performance vs. **Index** (Russell 2000, without dividends)

39.2%

31.2%

25.1%

18.8%

17.3%

19.3%

12.0%

8.8%

1 Year   3 Years   5 Years   10 Years

This chart for a Bankers Trust annual report does something I don't recommend unless the numbers let you stretch your humans without losing accuracy. The people here would look silly if the numbers were any smaller than the 18% shown, or more than 40% or 45%. In any case, only stretch one element of the person, and make the parts that mark percentages consistent across the chart. Using shadows gives you a second layer of plotting.
Art Director Melissa Makris..

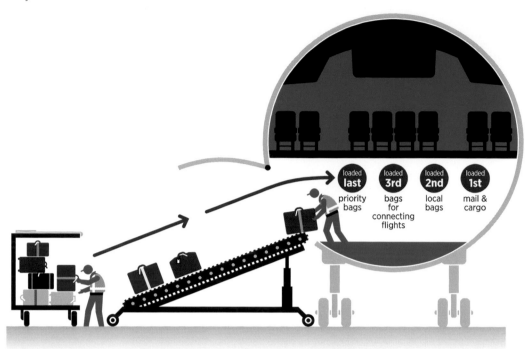

Above, adding humans to a simple graphic about the order of loading bags for US Airways magazine helps you realize what's going on while you are waiting to take off. Hopefully your precious holiday outfits are in the hands of baggage handlers who are in a good mood that day.

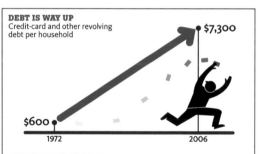

DEBT IS WAY UP
Credit-card and other revolving debt per household

$7,300

$600

1972   2006

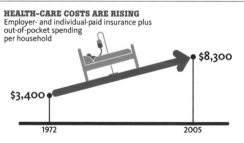

HEALTH-CARE COSTS ARE RISING
Employer- and individual-paid insurance plus out-of-pocket spending per household

$8,300

$3,400

1972   2005

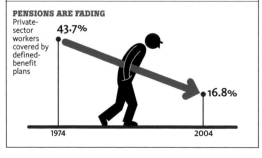

PENSIONS ARE FADING
Private-sector workers covered by defined-benefit plans

43.7%

16.8%

1974   2004

Left, when people interact with the graphic lines, you add info and emotion. These charts were for Money magazine

Opposite, for the Radio Times, I wanted to give a good sense of the size of the frightening obstacles encountered in three-day cross-country competitions, so I added the fearless horse and rider.

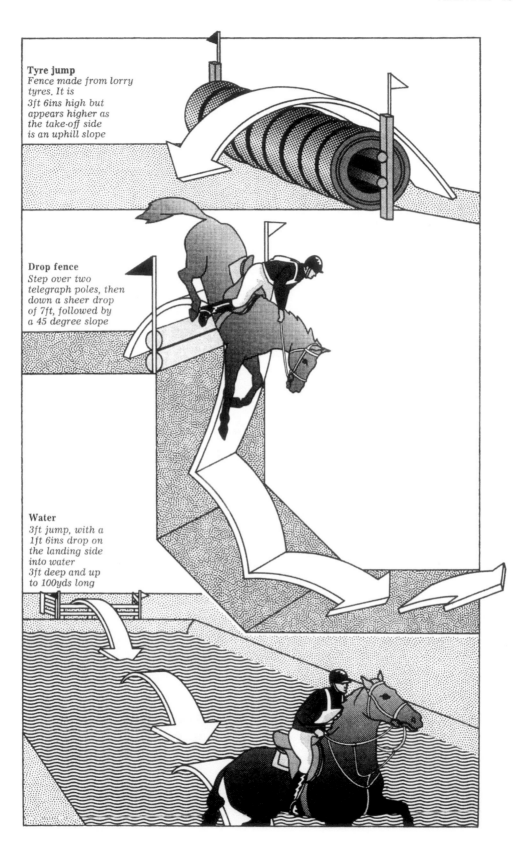

Tyre jump
Fence made from lorry tyres. It is 3ft 6ins high but appears higher as the take-off side is an uphill slope

Drop fence
Step over two telegraph poles, then down a sheer drop of 7ft, followed by a 45 degree slope

Water
3ft jump, with a 1ft 6ins drop on the landing side into water 3ft deep and up to 100yds long

#

Icons

Was this ☞ the first icon? The first map? 30-40,000 years ago, ☞ was a simple gesture that said: *the cave is that way.* (Cue a wink about it being the first 'digital' map.)

You can call this tiny pointing hand many things: icon, ideogram, symbol, sign, pictogram (in old typesetting shops, it was a *manicule,* or a 'printer's fist')—the names don't matter, but the icons themselves *do* matter; they are an essential part of infographic vocabulary. They are explanatory markers that, among other things, replace text.

Of course, early humans didn't have any text to replace. They spoke but didn't write. However, they could draw icons as well as anyone today. Look at the images of animals they made on the walls and ceilings of the Chauvet cave complex in France; they are uncannily similar to signs that warn today's drivers that animals might cross the road ahead. *(See the history chapter)*

The similarity shouldn't surprise us. Cave painters, and graphic designers thousands of years later, are after the same thing: the *essence* of the animal they are showing. The best, most direct, most clearly understood image of an animal—or almost anything—is a side view, and that's what is on cave walls and today's traffic signs. We are graphically linked to the cave painters.

The first symbol I was aware of was on the tins of petfood we gave our dog in the 1950s. (Spratts made a bird and a cat version, too.) It was the start of something small in my life—usually about an inch square.

I've done lots of icons. For an exhibition of my work at Stevenson University, the curator, Amanda Hostalka, needed a bold image to fill a space, so I gathered about 900 icons and symbols into a big poster, four feet across. *(Part of it is on the next page, greatly reduced.)* You can see that some groups of icons were designed as a set and used for a specific job, while others are arranged by subject matter: animals, people, transport, computers. I've used bits from those categories over and over in my graphics; they are part of a personal vocabulary— my own 'clip art.' It's a good habit, whenever you make a graphic with little pieces of art in it, to keep the pieces in labelled folders, so they can be used again. You'll change them subtly to make them exactly right for the particular reuse, but if you start from what you have already drawn you'll save tons of time and gradually build up your own icon arsenal of hearts, suns, clouds, cars, cats, and dogs, and you won't have to search (and pay) for clip art from the web that could appear—or could have already appeared—in someone else's work.

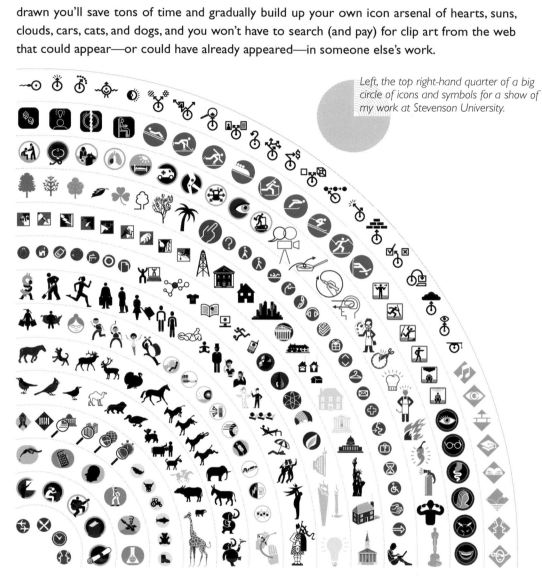

Left, the top right-hand quarter of a big circle of icons and symbols for a show of my work at Stevenson University.

The first symbolst I did were for the program pages of the *Radio Times,* which was the weekly magazine that listed everything on BBC radio and TV. Little black and white icons were used in the program pages as visual links from one mention of a radio or TV broadcast to another one airing the same subject at a different time of the day, like visual stepping stones. Most of them were for live sports coverage—ice skating, soccer, golf, and so on, *(below),* and every 4 years, for the BBC's coverage of the Olympic Games.

The Olympics have always produced their own official set of symbols, starting in earnest with the London Games in 1948. Olympic officials at those first post-war Games realized that they needed to have a common language to communicate with the athletes and visitors from the many nations taking part.

My favorite Olympic symbols were made by Katsumie Masuru and Yoshiro Yamashita, for Tokyo in 1964. This runner from the set *(below)* has wonderful energy.

Less aesthetically pleasing—less fun—but in the long run probably more influential, were the icons designed by Otl Aicher for the 1972 Munich Games, *(below)*. Aicher's associate, Heiner Jacob, said of their work: *'The Tokyo signs were a basis. However, they were constructed unsystematically ... for Munich there is a constant set of elements: a body alphabet (head, body, arms, and legs). The elements of this alphabet are arranged in a grid of four possible directions: horizontal, vertical, and two diagonal lines.'*

One of the reasons Aicher's symbol set was influential in the logo design world was precisely this grid. It was a kind of stick-man formula that gave designers a way to draw humans in sports and other logos without having to think too much. The icons were neat—and they did efficiently symbolize each Olympic sport—but they were cold.

So I was pleased to see that when the Games returned to Tokyo (delayed by Covid until 2021) their official symbol set, designed by Masaaki Hiromura, nodded nicely to Masuru's earlier, more human icons, *(right)*.

I think I'll go for a run myself. Mustn't forget to exercise!

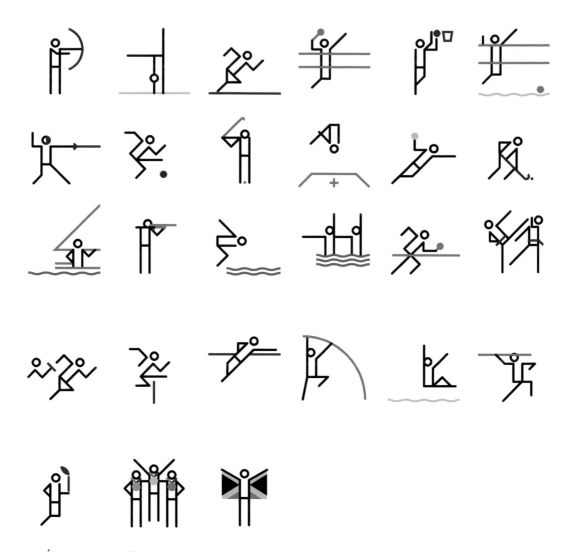

Álvaro Valiño's Olympic sports symbols for *The Washington Post, (above),* were drawn originally for the Rio Games in 2016, and updated for Tokyo with five new disciplines. While they use a strict organizing grid system like Aicher's Munich icons, these are light-hearted and warmly humanized.

On the web, they are animated, and Álvaro has added minimal sound effects that make you smile. It's a pity you can't *hear* them here. Have a look (and listen): https://www.alvarovalino.com/Olympic-pictograms

They look good on a coffee mug, too, and you can see frames from the animation sequence.

I like the winter symbols for the 1994 games in Lillehammer, Norway. Freelance designer and illustrator Sarah Rosenbaum based her icons *(right)* on a 4,000-year-old petroglyph from the Island of Tro in the north of the country. It was the first known image of a skier.

In 2016, the image was scratched over by a man trying to make it more visible for tourists visiting the site. (This is copied from what remains of the original.)

Unlike all previous Olympic symbols, Rosenbaum's were scratchy, almost childlike, doodles that didn't follow 'design' rules but perfectly matched the snowy Olympic locale. From the torch bearer to the crazy downhill skiers, they embodied the joyful spirit of the winter games in an original way.

In a 2005 interview by Farahnaz Mojtahedi for the Iranian graphic design magazine, Neshan, Sarah explained the genesis of her icons, while she worked in a small team of four, brought together by Petter Moshus, Design Director for the Lillehammer Games.

The brief said that the design should be 'true' and 'Norwegian,' so I went looking for things with actual historical reference. I came across a book about hieroglyphics in Norway (carvings in rock from the Bronze age). I looked at the squiggly figures and immediately thought they would make nice sports illustrations, and seemed to fit the strategic angle of the brief, having a link to 'true' history and a link to 'real', or natural material, like stone.

As soon as I started sketching from the images in the book, the idea of making pictograms from the figures seemed obvious. They were very clear and simple and nearly abstract in their form. There were several that could be used directly as sports pictograms with almost no alteration. The symbol that became the bobsled was one of these. It was as if it was an idea waiting to be found for this purpose. The concept of creating pictograms in the fashion of historical Norwegian stone carvings was an idea I brought to the first meeting of the group of designers, which comprised Knut Harlem, Reidar Holtskog, and Åsmund Sand, as well as me. In the end it took me about three days to draw each pictogram, using two kinds of pens, and working quite small—only an inch or two high. The effect that the edge of the ink made on paper resembled the uneven structure of the stone in the original hieroglyphics.

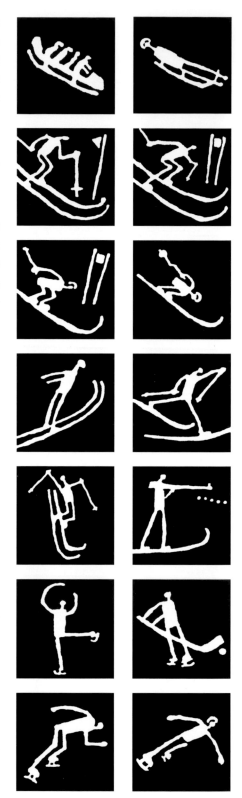

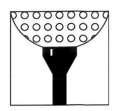

Lillehammer showed that it was OK for Oympic symbols to be fun. But designers beware! Icons can be misunderstood. Readers wrote to the *Radio Times* objecting to a golf symbol of mine. They thought it was a closeup of a crotch. People will see what they want to see. It's a good idea to show a friend—not a designer—what you've drawn, and ask what they think your image represents, and what else it might possibly be.

Some people think that my work includes unnecessary "embellishments," (others call it *chart junk*), but the design of icons is one area where I think stripping away unnecessary 'junk' is the right thing to do. Despite my dislike of clichés, icons are usually a kind of cliché—an idea honed down to its absolute and obvious minimum. In the 1920's, while he was developing *Isotype,* Otto Neurath instructed the artists making icons for his charts to cut the images out of black paper, forcing them to simplify images so as not to get bogged down in unnecessary surface detail. When artist Gerd Arntz joined the team, he didn't need to be told how to simplify an image—it was exactly what he had been doing all along with his linoleum cuts, which Otto had seen at an exhibition in 1923. Gerd changed the way Otto's team made icons—from paper-cutting to linoleum-cutting—a move that had the added benefit of printing multiple copies of the images from the cut lino.

But no matter how they were produced, Neurath was right to insist that his graphics team find the visual *essence* of the icon they were drawing. And for that, choosing the best view of the subject was important. This was more often than not a silhouette, or side view. Design historian Ellen Lupton has described this approach as 'pre-chemical photography,' and Neurath did suggest that his artists look at the flat shadow that an object cast, and draw *that,* instead of the object itself.

The Italian archeologist Emmanuel Anati (born 1930) has proposed that early humans could identify animal and human tracks in snow. He said that they learned to 'read' before they could write. Neurath's profiles and silhouettes (and shadows) were like Anati's footprints—they were 'reflections' of reality—documentary evidence, left behind by the real thing.

The *Isotype* system was more than a method of lining up icons in rows to make pictorial bar charts. Neurath put two icons together to make a third: by combining an image of a person with an image of an i-beam, he made a steelworker. That same image of a person with a loaf of bread added became a baker.

As with many clever ideas, this seems obvious to us today.

Much of the icon work that Arntz did for Neurath—the surface look of it—is mimicked today, and the graphic principles behind *Isotype* are often overlooked. But this chapter is about the symbols, rather than their application to a system of chartmaking that uses countable pictorial units; and Arntz's drawings are such beautiful observations of whatever he was symbolizing, it is easy to be seduced into copying his style, even if we have to update some of his images of cars and phones. I'm sure that a good deal of the success of *Isotype*—and its current revival—is because of the friendly look of Arntz's contributions. Most of the symbols that he made 80 years ago look fresh today.

In his efforts to be both pictorially interesting and statistically accountable, Neurath wanted the icons to be neutral, or deadpan. But it's hard not to have sympathy for Arntz's huddled, unemployed man, *(right),* or feel the weight of the box this guy is carrying, *(far right).* The reason these images by Arntz (redrawn here) are effective is that they were the product of close observation by someone who was an artist first and a graphic designer second. However simply executed, we still enjoy looking at them, and recognizing the humanity in such tiny pictures.

Emojis

Stripping away everything but the absolute graphic essentials when designing icons has hit a brick wall with the déluge of emojis. What started as emoticons (emotional icons)—that is, punctuation marks and other typographic characters arranged in a combination of keystrokes to make pictures of faces, such as the famous smiley face :-) or this wink ;-) or Santa Claus *<|:o)> —has ballooned into thousands of separate emojis today. (The word emoji doesn't stem from emotion, it comes from the Japanese words for image, pronounced eh, and character, pronounced moji.)

Faces made out of punctuation first appeared in *Puck Magazine* in **1881** *(below).* The modern versions were invented by Scott Fahlman in **1982**. According to Pagan Kennedy, writing in *The New York Times Magazine*, Fahlman's smiley face :-) was intended 'to take the sting out of mocking statements' and other differences of opinion on online forums. He called his invention a joke marker.

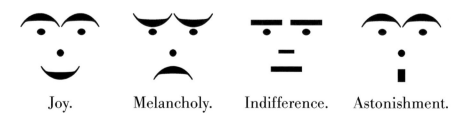

Joy.   Melancholy.   Indifference.   Astonishment.

In 1993, Tota Enomoto published *Niko! [Smile!] The Smiley Collection,* with 200 emoticons you could read without tilting your head sideways. Compared to western keyboards, there are many more characters available on Japanese keyboards, so pictures of faces can be horizontal.

But soon, five or six—or even just three—keystrokes, like Fahlman's :-) proved to be too much for people who wanted to add a tiny picture to their email and text messages. Enter the emoji. One touch on the keyboard and there was a picture. The first examples are often credited to Shigetaka Kurita. They are enshrined at New York's Museum of Modern Art. *(Below, the installation.)* Kurita created 176 characters for the Japanese phone company NTT Docomo, in the i-mode division, in 1998 and 1999. (Docomo stands for 'DO Communications Over MObile network.' Also, Dokomo means 'everywhere' in Japanese.)

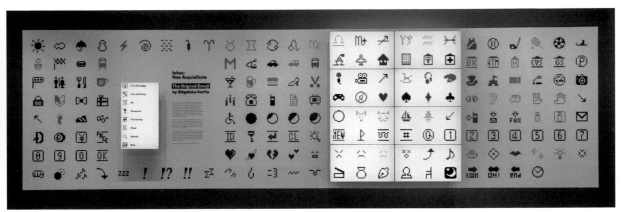

However, in 1997, another Japanese company, SoftBank (called J-phone at the time), produced a set of 90 emojis for their Skywalker DP-211SW model. These were the first emojis designed for mobile phones. In 2019, Shigetaka Kurita himself acknowledged as much in a tweet. As of this writing, the designer of the SoftBank emojis is unknown.

In 2010, emojis were added to the International Unicode Consortium, a non-profit group of programmers who standardized the coding of fonts so that computers and phones all talk to each other in the same way. With the release of Emoji 14.0 in September 2021, there are now roughly 3,600 emoji characters on the Unicode list. It's a big number partly because many human faces are pictured in a range of different skin tones. You can look them all up on emojipedia.org.

I understand the intent to create racial and gender equality in emojis. However, I fear that eventually there'll be such a glut of images, designed to cater to everyone while offending no one, that we will be overwhelmed by the massive choice, and I wonder if we might inadvertently make some racial or gender mistake in a text or other message. What happened to the idea of making symbolic instead of pictorial, literal, images? Perhaps, for no better reason that emojis are tiny, they are considered to be the same thing as symbols. They are not.

I sent a screen shot of the 200 (!) different emojis that can be used to represent a 'couple' to my granddaughter, Kai, (aged 16 at the time) who replied: '*I think it's great to see the inclusivity, but ya I'd have to agree it's a bit much when you type each of them out. I personally was very happy to see the non-binary emojis added, including couple ones, but I can't rly speak for POC on how POC emojis being added might've felt. It's a nice feeling when you see something that represents you in such a small thing like emojis. Again, when you type each of them out it does seem exaggerated, but (to me) so do all the food emojis, or the different type of trains. They don't take up much space, it's set up so you can kinda customize your own couple, but I do see how people could see it as too much.*'

It's a touchy subject. But regardless of the color of our skin, or hair, or haircut, or sexual difference we are all PEOPLE first. Most variations of the original smiley face are still available in yellow—i.e., not race- or gender-based—but now you have your choice of different skin tone, hair color, beard. Symbolically speaking, I don't think we need all the available tiny pictures of police officers. They are no longer symbols when there's so much pictorial detail in them. This one from Docomo is just fine. ■

And *symbols* are what I'm going on about here. Empathy and inclusion is important in infographics and I have addressed that in the section about adding humans and humanity to your graphics.

When making icons of people for *Isotype*-like charts, consider making them blue. Using a blue figure of a person is not a way to avoid questions of difference or inequality, it simply makes everyone equal, whereas showing people in precisely color-calibrated, almost-realistic, pictures amplifies the differences—that's the intention, of course—but it does not promote equality. Our western alphabet has 26 letters, and it's pretty good at giving us many ways to say what we want to say; will 3,600 (and counting) emojis ever become an efficient way to communicate equality, as we abandon words and fall deeper into the language of texting, hunting through the pile for the right shade of skin or hair color, or hair length, not to mention the person's age, physical appearance, and the right uniform for the job? No, 3,600 will never be enough.

BBBBBUT, I hear you say, don't emojis lighten up written language? Isn't that exactly the sort of joyful thing this book is all about? My argument has less to do with the realistic look of emojis—although I do prefer simpler graphic versions—it has more to do with the attempt to become a language desperately aiming to include everyone. *Symbols* already include everyone.

Strings of emojis or emoticons aren't a new language. They are messages that are not completely spelled out—they are inferred—your eye reads part of them. You learn the code as you go along, and your friends learn your message-language, your use of emojis, which have different meanings for different people. Here's Kai again, in response to my asking this: Why do you use :) and not a yellow smiley face emoji at the end of your text message? Are emojis out of fashion? Kai: 'I tend to use :) :(>:) and such as more general emojis. The others I'll use to help specify or exaggerate a tone I'm using … I wouldn't say emojis are out of fashion exactly, just being used differently. It also varies from person to person, it's a stylistic choice in the end. Also, in my case at least, It's faster to type it out, instead of having to look for a specific one.'

By the way, >:) is a devilish smile. Kai says: 'if hahaha is :) then hehehe is >:)'

Emojis are fun, but they are not a language. I mean, try reading *Emoji Dick*; it's a version of *Moby Dick* that replaces all Melville's words with emojis. The creator, Fred Benenson, prints the text, too. Here's the famous first line: ☎ 😶 🔺 🐦 👌 Have fun 'reading' it!

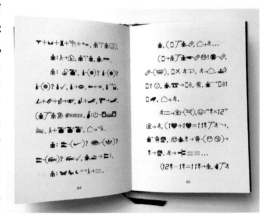

That said, there is one book that consists entirely of emojis, symbols, and icons that I happily recommend: *Book from the Ground: from point to point*, by Xu Bing, 2013 *(right)*, a graphic novel that describes 24 hours in the life of an urban white-collar worker. I knew this was what the book was about before I started to 'read' it because it helpfully says so on the back cover—the only place where any words appear. It's a beautifully designed book, and while the simple plot description is welcome, the graphic thinking inside is clear, and ultimately the story is a pleasure to read—albeit a little slow—so it was hardly necessary to explain the idea.

Xu Bing says: '*Twenty years ago I made Book from the Sky, a book of illegible Chinese characters that no one could read. Now I have created Book from the Ground, a book that anyone can read. Though quite different, the two books share something in common: regardless of a reader's language or level of education, the books treat all readers equally. Book from the Sky was an expression of doubt and alarm regarding preexisting systems of writing; Book from the Ground expresses the ideal of a single, universally understood language, and my sense of the direction of contemporary communication.*'

Linguists, designers, social scientists, teachers, and a 12th century nun, among hundreds (yes, hundreds!) of others, have invented what they hoped would be internationally understood languages. None have lasted. *Esperanto* (by Ludwik Zamenhof, 1887) came closest; *Klingon* (by Marc Okrand, 1984) survives as a pop curiosity for devoted Star Trek followers. JRR Tolkein's passion for invented languages led him to construct grammars and vocabularies for *Elvish*, among many other languages in his books.

Tolkein was a calligrapher and he created scripts to go along with his inventions, but very few invented languages were pictorial, and those that were have not fared any better than their purely alphabetic cousins.

Three picture languages have come the closest to success: Charles Bliss's *Semantography* from 1949, *(top right)*—Bliss later named it *Blissymbolics*; Yukio Ota's *LoCoS (Lovers' Communication System)* from 1964, *(bottom right);* and Otto Neurath's *Isotype* from the 1920s. Unlike the first two, Neurath never claimed that he had invented a total language; he called it a 'helping language' rather than a complete substitute for the written word.

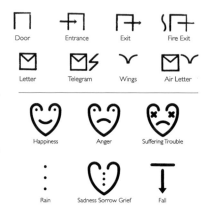

Neurath had the right idea, and linguist Neil Cohn has written that there will never be a universal visual language, certainly not one called *Emoji*. Put simply, we use different spoken and written languages in the world because we come from different cultures. It's even more apparent with icons, symbols, pictures. Cohn: '*…people who do not have cultural exposure to images often have difficulty understanding the meaning of images.*' Different cultures see things differently.

But let's speculate! If a truly universal picture language could ever be created, it's a fair guess that it would be on your phone. 80% of people in the world have a smart phone—that's 6.5 billion people—and it's the way we communicate, like it or not. Today, tap 'thank you' into *Google Translate* when writing to a friend in Germany, and get 'danke' back in an instant. Perhaps tomorrow there'll be a device that translates any language into pictograms—flat and symbolic, I hope—drawn from a huge visual vocabulary that encompasses all cultural differences. I said it would be a huge vocabulary, but, hey, computers are good at handling that sort of thing. However, even if we assume that Neil Cohn's warning about cultural misunderstandings is taken care of, there is a reason for *not* doing this: if the point is clear communication, we can already use artificially intelligent earbuds to translate conversations while we speak and listen (and interrupt). Why do we need pictures at all?

For joy, that's why! For fun, and to soften that email; to wink, to say something visually that we can't quite say in words. Emojis are good at that. They are Neurath's 'helping language.'

I was glad when Apple changed its operating system icons—the ones for phone, music, messages, mail, etc.—from 3-d renderings to simpler, flattened images. The old style was called skeuomorphism, which referred to icons that were practically photographs of what was being depicted—trashcans or file folders, for instance. The change happened around 2013, when other big corporations were similarly flattening their logos; the iconic Volkswagen VW in a circle became starkly simple, losing its reflective, beveled edges that cast deep shadows. Similarly, Nissan, Toyota, Intel, PBS, Warner Bros., and Burger King, and others simplified their logos. Today, emojis are in flux, design-wise. Those tiny fully-rendered portraits of people and animals and everything else, with their 3-d shadows and shiny surfaces remain on some platforms, but Microsoft's Windows 11 Fluent emojis are now 2-d, while Apple's IOS icons have crept back into the color gradation and shadow game.

This is my humble plea for future emoji designers: instead of little pictures, let's use symbols—simple symbols—that get to the essence of the person or thing, and that don't try to be realistic renderings. Check out Noto Emoji; a nice start—in glorious black and white!

Smile!

Graphic designer Art Chantry tried to discover the origin of the happy, or smiley face—the forerunner of the most well-known emoji. Chantry's graphic digging is a chapter in Steve Heller's book *I Heart Design*. Many people have claimed they were the inventor of the smiley face. Often cited is graphic designer Harvey Ross Ball who drew a round yellow face with dark eyes and wide smiling mouth for State Mutual Life Assurance Company of Worcester, Mass, in 1963, to be used on buttons, cards and posters. It took him 10 minutes, and he was paid $45.

The most joyful—and easily the largest—version I know of is in the Douglas fir forest in Oregon, where David Hampton, owner of Hampton Lumber, planted larch trees that turn brown each fall and make a 300-ft happy face, *(right)*.

In the end, Chantry's answer to who invented the happy face is that…*'every little girl who dotted her i with a smiley face is the author. Every person who slaps a smiley emoticon onto their comment on a blog or email is the author. Every ad agency hack who thinks they invented the concept of a smiling little face is the author. We are all the author. The happy face basically grew on a tree. Maybe a cherry tree.'*

Sounds right. 'Cherry tree' refers to The Cherry Hut, a store in Beulah, Michigan, founded in 1922, whose logo is (still) a cherry-red happy face.

Smiley afterthoughts
Amazon neatly encapsulates its business with an underline 'smile' from A to Z in its logo. Too bad when a package lands upside down on your porch, and it's scowling at you.

And why does Hyatt have a growling mouth in its logo? Don't they want to put on a happy face to greet you in their hotels?

Will you be my Valentine?

Where did the heart shape come from? Visually, it's a stretch from the bloody throbbing blob in our chest. What happened, graphically? Three theories....

It's an image of the silphium seedpod. Silphium, a type of fennel, was critical to the economy of the Greek colony of Cyrene, in the 7th century B.C. It was thought to be a contraceptive, and became associated with sex. It was so popular that they put the modern heart-shaped image of the seed on their coins.

Cupid and the idea of romantic love took hold of the Medieval imagination in the 1400s; the heart shape was seen as the head of Cupid's arrow with the pointy parts rounded.

Upside down, it's the shape of a butt. Hmmm.

<3

Who needs a theory when you can tap out a nice emoticon?

It's said that the heart icon is a nothing but a botched drawing of the real anatomy. But look: it's not *that* botched—here's an old engraving, and my heart diagram from *Mortality*.

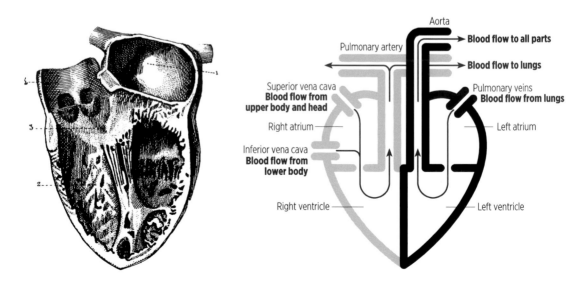

The best use of the heart icon is Milton Glaser's much copied *I [Heart] New York,* famously first scribbled in the back of a taxi. This is a whole page from *The New York Times* on September 14th, 2001. At the very bottom, you can see the sponsor using a heart in their own tagline.

September 11, 2001. Our hearts go out to you. **VIRGINIA IS FOR LOVERS**

Showing the way

You've seen Paul Mijksenaar's wayfinding icons and maps if you have flown into or out of many of the world's airports. His first airport job was for Schiphol, Amsterdam, in 1990. Here are some of the many symbols he and his team produced.

Paul always thinks of the traveler first, and his humor shines through his work. When he found out that car owners had trouble reconnecting with their cars in Schiphol's numbered parking facilities, he commissioned Dutch cartoonist Opland to draw 'visual reminders' for

each section and floor of the three huge parking lots. If you parked your car in the 'Holland' section, you went there and then followed the windmill or cow or clogs signs, *(right).*

Voila! (Or whatever that is in Dutch—a notoriously difficult language, and thus all the more reason for international wayfinding signs.) In 2012, Opland's original black and white drawings were redrawn, in color, by Max Kisman.

Paul's good humor as the overall designer of signage at Schiphol, is also evident in the oft-imitated fly in the urinal symbol. The man in charge of toilet cleaning at the airport, Jos van Bedaf, had the idea of putting a drawing of a fly in the urinal bowls, to prompt men to aim better, *(right).*

Paul Mijksenaar makes travel easier when you might be stressed, and more friendly when you might feel like a herded animal. That's why he's included here as a joyful *infografisto.*

Turning language into pictures—literally

Luigi Farrauto used to work in the Mijksenaar office. For this project—it was his dissertation thesis, and it got him the job with Paul—Luigi first designed a modern Arabic typeface, then used the shapes of the letterforms to 'draw' buildings and places in Damascus, in the same way that this :-) is a face. Luigi's icons are typographic pictures of destinations *(the lighter blue squares, right).* Arabic speakers may be able to read

الكنيسة المريمية   Mariamiya Church

حمام الملك الظاهر   Hammam al-Malik al-Dhahir

قصر العظم   Azem Palace

باب صغير   Bab Saghir

سوق القطن   Suq al-Qouton

مطعم بيت جبري   Jabri House

fragments of Arabic words in these typographic pictures, while tourists can sense the Arabic 'feel'—seeing the pictures as part of the signs (which include the name of the café, mosque, sauna, or souk in English). An arrow points pedestrians and drivers in the right direction. It's signage that adds a light touch to the street, with a nice flavor of the city.

Like Luigi Farrauto's Arabic-based pictures of buildings, other written languages that don't use the Roman alphabet can be 'translated' by turning their letterforms into pictures in order to understand their meaning.

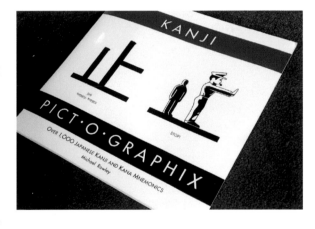

Some of these languages were pictorial in the first place—Japanese kanji characters for instance, evolved into abstract shapes from the picture-language of ancient China.

Michael Rowley drew friendly visual mnemonics of Japanese characters for his 1992 book, *Kanji Pict-o-graphix, (above).* In the introduction, he explains that Japanese schoolchildren learn by writing each kanji hundreds of times at their desks. He continues: *'If you are not a Japanese schoolchild, you probably do what I did: stare at each one and make up a story that you can mentally 'attach' to the kanji to help you recall its meaning when you meet it again.'* Michael's book has a over a thousand kanji explanations—about half of all kanji characters in general use in Japan.

In this chapter, we've looked at signs, icons, symbols, pictograms—what we call them doesn't matter. How well they communicate ideas does.

Next pages: a gallery of icons.

Earlier in this chapter, I showed you Álvaro Valiño's Olympic icons. Here's his set of icons for the Rundfunk Symphony Orchestra Berlin.

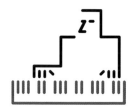

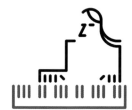

From the conductor to the triangle player, they are wonderfully simple images of classical musicians playing their instruments.

Álvaro comments on the job:

'At first, I was a bit shocked that they contacted me from a Symphonic orchestra. I have to confess I don't know much about classical music, but I truly love the effect it produces on me, mind and body... everytime I go to a concert.

This project is a cousin of my Olympics work for The Washington Post in its formal flavor. The communications people at the Symphony orchestra weren't happy with any of their existing visual repertoire—visual voice, logo, typography, images—they wanted to change everything.

So I started working with them around the idea of forgetting the logo and making these evolved iconic illustrations into their visual language. The lines, the color, the playful but clean spirit...They are very happy with this approach.'

Álvaro continued this visual language with posters, booklets, programs, and composer portraits; Beethoven is over there on the right.

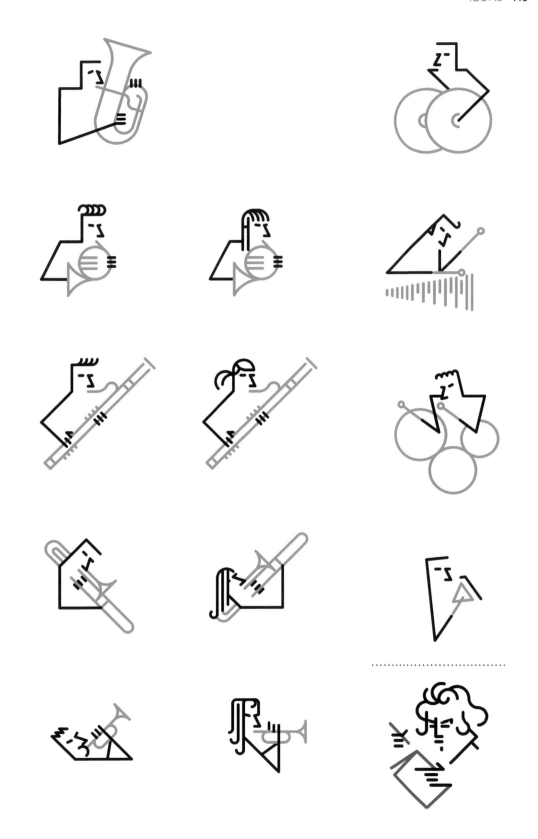

beauty & body

IN WHICH **AISLE** CAN I FIND...?

Richard Saul Wurman was hired by the pharmacy chain CVS to organize their stores. He wanted everything to be centered on the human body. A graphic, (left) showed shoppers where to find different products.

Below, a different approach (Here, the Spanish version.)

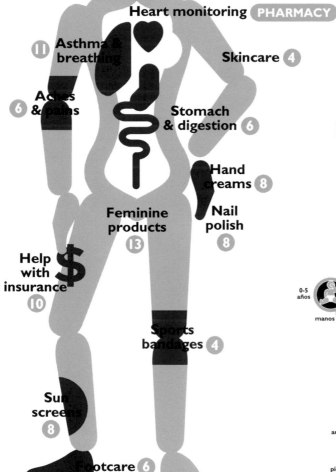

9 Haircare

Eyecare 12

Makeup 8

Ear, nose & mouth products
5 6

Prescriptions PHARMACY

Heart monitoring PHARMACY

11 Asthma & breathing

Skincare 4

6 Aches & pains

Stomach & digestion 6

Hand creams 8

Feminine products
13

Nail polish
8

Help with insurance
10

$

Sports bandages 4

Sun screens
8

Footcare 6

belleza & cuerpo

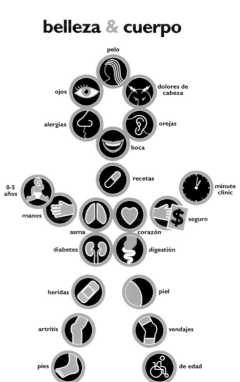

pelo

ojos

dolores de cabeza

alergias

orejas

boca

0-5 años

recetas

minute clinic

manos

seguro

asma

corazón

diabetes

digestión

heridas

piel

artritis

vendajes

pies

de edad

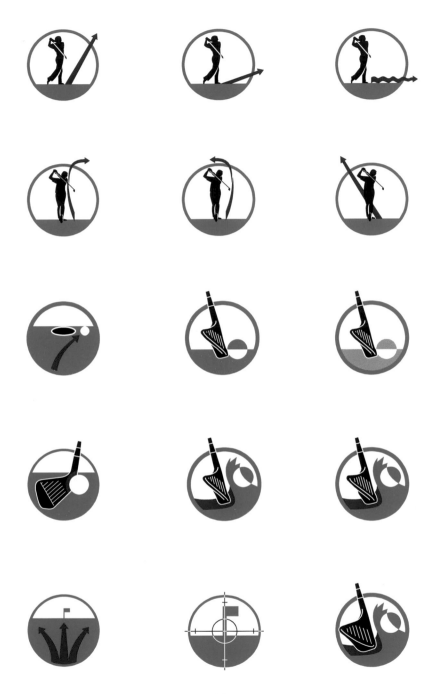

For Golf Digest magazine, part of a set of 22 icons for the section that dispensed help with your swing and other problems, showing many of the different clubs used. (Art Director Ina Saltz)

Above and below, for a project directed by RKC!, these are two versions of a set of icons for Smithfield Farms.

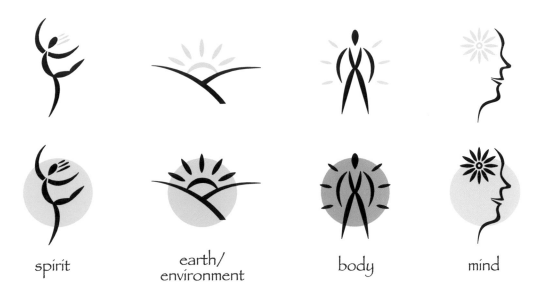

spirit   earth/environment   body   mind

The photographer Kwaku Alston had an idea for a yoga app. These are two slightly different looks at 'section' headings. Although they are basically stick figures, I wanted a softer, more fluid feel.

For the Mexican Yellow Pages phone directory, Richard Saul Wurman asked me to design a set of icons for the different category listings.

ICONS for BPP app
August 2014

 = no/don't   = reduce

bike/walk

use public transportation

turn lights off

bring own cup

clothes washer/dryer full load

take shopping bag to store

share cooking and eating meals

participate in community gardens

carpool

use less water

use cloth rags

full load dish washer

buy from farmer's market

use natural cleaning products

print both sides

recycle daily items

switch to e-bills

no air conditioning in car

compost

dry on clothesline

use thermostat to regulate heating/cooling

no meat day

local beer/beverage day

no soda pop

plant native low-water plants

collect rainwater for plants

turn off tap when brushing teeth

no water at restaurants if not drinking it

put bricks in toilet tank

flush less

check for leaks

turn off computer

use dish water to flush toilet

replace inefficient windows

insulate and caulk house

buy hybrid/alt. fuel car

save cold water from shower to water plants or flush

heat/cool only necessary rooms

close curtains to cool house

open windows to cool down

support clean water initiatives

use stairs

enroll in carshare program

walk the dog

spay/neuter pet

recycle aluminum, steel and wood

take local vacations

choose an energy star fridge

replace top-loading machines

check faucets for leaks

AIR

WATER

LAND

FOOD

LEADERBOARD

Above, Stanford magazine published a big feature on all aspects of recycling at the University, in 2019. These photographic-plus-stickmen icons went with items about recyling food scraps, plastic, electronics, paper, construction and landscaping materials. (Art Director Bambi Nicklen).

In 2014, Della van Heyst started the Billion People Project, a smartphone-based way to record personal recycling activities and habits, to post the results and compare one's efforts to others'. Left, the complete set of icons, actual size; what they look like on a smartphone; below, the logo.

1,ᵢᵢᵢ,ᵢᵢᵢ,ᵢᵢᵢ

These single-line drawings (with a few dots) were for Network World magazine. Some imagery gets outdated fast…

…this is what desktop computers looked like in 2000.

…remember pagers?

Art Director Caroline Bowyer asked me for a set of symbols for different departments in This Old House magazine.

George W. helped navigate the intricacies of how the government works for Kids Discover magazine.
(Art Directors Mary K. Baumann and Will Hopkins)

For Condé Nast's first prototype of a new financial magazine—the working
title was Currency—I drew a little money person to animate the pages.
(Art Director Tom Bentkowski)

A set of symbols for Vanity Fair magazine in 2006 about the way
politically red states had higher rates of deaths by guns, incarceration,
female incarceraton, divorce, illegitimacy, suicide, obesity, and executions.

For Details magazine in 2002, these were questions to ask before a
blind date: Do you have body piercings? Long hair? Smoker? Drinker?
How old are you? Do you go skinny dipping? Are you tattooed?

Icons for sections of the Industry Standard. (Art Director Bob Ciano)

Logos for Neoptix, a sunglass manufacturer.

Today, many logos are abstract, geometric shapes. Businesses think they need a mark that's abstract enough to include all possible new acquisitions or changes to their line of work. The logo for Meta, the umbrella name for Facebook and its offshoots, is an example of this. It's a variation of the mathematical symbol for infinity, which has been around for a long time.

 The infinity symbol, invented by an English maths guy, John Wallis, in 1655

About their version of infinity, Mark Zuckerberg's design team is quoted as saying that the new logo *'is designed to grow and change with the company as the metaverse is created.'*

Does this mean designers have to make their logos as bland and meaningless as possible so *anything* can be read into them at *any* time in the future? What a pity. Wit should have a place in the boardroom. A smile can help in many ways—people remember logos or symbols because they are amused or intrigued, or simply because they can see something (or themselves) in it.

One picture is worth a thousand abstractions.

And if there's a human in the picture, probably two thousand.

   To see the symbols and icons clearly in this chapter, I've enlarged most of them. When designing symbols, don't forget that many will be tiny when they appear in print. These refugee icons are designed to be used at this small size on maps. (They show refugees from three different time periods: with a bundle carried on the back from long ago; with a suitcase during mid-20th century; with a wheeled suitcase from today.) A question arises about the gender of such people depicted: are all stick figures men? In a war, it's more likely that the people who are fleeing will be women and children (the men are fighting), so should that be reflected in the icon? Or can icons like that just represent people, regardless of their gender?

Joyful presentations

The annual Stanford Professional Publishing Course (SPPC), where I taught from 1980 to 2009, was where I learned how to play with different ways to present information, and get the audience to play along with me. In the 1980s, the SPPC lasted two weeks and included 70-odd lectures. After a first intense week that was all about writing, editing, and copyright law, people were understandably exhausted, and needed a breathing space. So, when the weekend came along it was the turn of the 'art department'—illustration, typography, photography, art direction, and myself on information graphics. We were no less intense, but the teaching experience for attendees felt different, moving from Stanford classrooms to a campus theater auditorium with a huge screen where we could show off our images. And a backstage! Here I could hide all sorts of props.

Over the years, these included a life size, flat construction of a horse with moveable legs to demonstrate Muybridge's proof that all four hooves are off the ground at certain times while galloping; a full set of drums; and three helium-filled weather balloons that unspooled rolls of toilet paper printed with dollar bills to make a wall-sized bar chart of money. *(See next page.)*

Della van Heyst, the organizer and first host of the course, gently pushed me to try different approaches to making presentations. Back home in Westport, Connecticut, I enlisted the help of my wife's stepfather, Lenny Stea, a sound engineer, who had a recording studio there. Lenny made me cassette tapes (remember those?) of sound effects, snippets of music—as well as audience applause and laughter, in case there wasn't any—to use in the talks. Later, we did everything digitally and it was much easier to cue up the sounds.

Della, and her successor Holly Brady, always made sure that there would be time for me to set up and rehearse some of the more extreme effects in the auditorium, with no audience there. I usually did this with the help of a wonderful Stanford audio-visual technician, Guy Bailey, whose patience while I set up my stuff, seeing what was going to work and what wasn't, was as much of a help as I could possibly have had. Make friends with the AV team!

Rehearsal is important. Not just knowing the order of your slides—although that's essential, too. If you don't prepare, and aren't sure what the next slide is while you are lecturing, your

MY PRESENTATION OF HOW MUYBRIDGE WON A BET FOR HIS SPONSOR, LELAND STANFORD

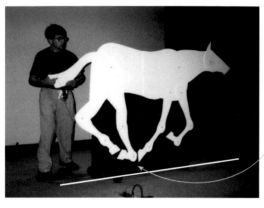

Stanford wanted to show his colleagues that all four hooves are off the ground at one time during a gallop.

Sorry about the quality of this photo! (Also, this angle makes the shapes look odd)

The horse was built in separate parts using lightweight foamcore, in my studio in Connecticut, and assembled at the conference.

First, the whole horse was drawn...

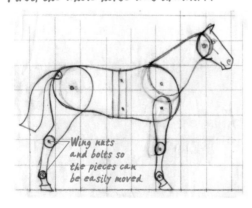

Wing nuts and bolts so the pieces can be easily moved.

...then outlines of the parts were transferred to the foamcore sheets.

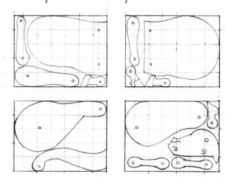

presentation comes across as a self-centered portfolio show. *'Oh, yes, and then I did this...'* doesn't sound professional when you are surprised by an image you had forgotten you had included. And if you attempt something beyond a standard PowerPoint show that is just you talking with pictures projected next to you, rehearsal is even more important.

Some live presentations were performed versions of charts I'd already done in print. One of these was showing how many hot dogs are eaten at the annual Hot Dog Eating Contest at Coney Island, New York. I had become obsessed with how Takeru Kobayashi managed to eat 50 of them. (That was in 2001; subsequent years saw that number eclipsed, and the record

RAISING THE $64,000 WALL OF MONEY

If I'm lucky, someone takes pictures during my talk. (They might be blurry!)

Helium weather balloons lift up · · · · · ·

rolls of toilet paper printed with dollar bills

When fully lifted up, this is $64,000
For that money you could buy:

• a toilet in a house in Honolulu
(average cost: $764,000 in December 2021)
and use this paper in it for quite a long time.

• half a square inch of Van Gogh's 1890 painting, Dr. Gachet
(24 × 22 inches; sold for $82.5 million at auction in 1990)

---

set by Joey Chestnut in 2021 is now 76 hot dogs—eaten in 10 minutes. My question was how to show that amount of not-very-good-for-you-processed meat. Clearly, my demonstration would fall short of the real-life event, but I could explain the eating technique that Takeru developed and which most competitive eaters now use.

It's this: dunk the bun into a glass of water, and stuff it down your throat using the hotdog as a kind of plunger. Repeat 50 times. I did it with just one hotdog, then put on an xxx-large t-shirt with images of hotdogs sewn onto it. I stuffed a pillow up the t-shirt. The result was a sort of silly x-ray of my stomach. One fun-loving conference organizer in Holland had 52 hot dogs cooked and brought onto the stage to show the quantity consumed by the most recent competition's winner; it was nice to be able to hand them out to the first few rows of the audience, *(right).*

HOW TO TO EAT 52 HOT DOGS

It's a messy business

Takeru's dunking technique

Hot dog-eating contest winners end up with this many in their stomachs!

I asked John Grimwade, well-known for lively and inventive infographic in-person lectures, to tell me a bit about his approach to making presentations:

'I've usually started presentations with a little humor, to break the ice and to make it clear that I don't take myself too seriously. Sometimes, depending on the subject and audience, I've included quite a few light-hearted elements spread throughout a lecture. Of course, it's a well-established way to engage people, but is much more effective if the humorous parts of a presentation relate in some way to the rest of the content.'

John added two warnings from his experience:

• We're not professional entertainers.
'There's always the lurking danger of straying into what I call 'stand-up comedy territory.' Humorous items that do not reference the general theme are not going to add to the credibility of a lecture. And yes, I admit, I've made this mistake several times myself, through nervousness, or a worry that the audience isn't going to be interested in the material I'm presenting.'

• Know your audience
'While humor can be a definite asset, it also has the potential to fall flat, and then you wish you hadn't attempted it. The comment or image (or both) that you thought would bring the house down, is not understood at all, and is followed by an uneasy silence. This possibility is something to carefully consider when preparing your lecture. There's no easy answer to this, but if in doubt, err on the side of caution.'

John's point about not being professional entertainers is important. Sometimes I've felt that I have been asked to lecture as though I am one, and this is because conference organizers are happy to temper the more obviously serious lectures in their agenda with a lighter one. If the title of your presentation is *Can Humor be Appropriate in Information Design?* you are expected to deliver some fun!

Make sure that your content has a serious intent in there somewhere, even if it's delivered with a light touch. Invite a few people up from the audience and get them to help you construct a live chart in front of their fellow attendees. This both amuses and informs. It's what I call performance graphics, and it includes two of the main points about joyful infographics: context, and, obviously, audience.

There's an old Chinese proverb:

Tell me and I'll forget; show me and I may remember;
involve me and I'll understand.

This is an audience involvement piece I've given a few times.

Million, Billion, Trillion

Before this lecture, I printed signs big enough to be seen at the back of any large meeting room. The signs read 1,000,000; 1,000,000,000; and 1,000,000,000,000.

Did you have to think a bit before you said million, billion and trillion to yourself? All those zeros are part of the problem. When it came to this part of the talk, I invited six people to come up and join me on the 'stage.' I explained that together we were going to set up a timeline, measured in years.

The timeline started with 'today' at one end, had a midpoint of 16,000 years ago, and finished with 32,000 years ago at the other end. (The wider the stage the better.) Three participants stood at these points. Next, I handed out the signs. One of the remaining three participants got the 'million' sign, a second got the 'billion,' and a third the 'trillion.' I told them that these numbers represented a million seconds, a billion seconds, and a trillion seconds, and that we were going to plot where each of these numbers fell on the timeline we had just made.

Not many people know how long a million seconds is, let alone a billion or a trillion. I have friendly fun asking the audience and the person holding the 1,000,000 sign. There are wild guesses about where he or she should stand on the timeline. The answer: a million seconds is 12 days. I ask the 1,000,000 sign-holder to stand 12 days away from the person who's standing at 'today.' Considering that the three human markers on the timeline are 16,000 years apart, it's almost impossible for the person with the million sign to stand close enough to 'today.' But it's fun to watch them try.

Next, the sign for a billion seconds. Where is that on our timeline? A billion seconds is 32 years. Again, given the scale of years we have set up, this number is also very close to 'today.' There's more fun as three people now try to stand on virtually the same spot.

Finally, a trillion seconds. By this time, there's often someone in the audience who sees what I'm getting at. If a billion seconds is 32 years, then a trillion is 32,000 years. Three more zeros. The person holding that sign walks right past the 16,000-year mark to the far end of the timeline. What's left for the audience to see is a million (seconds) and a billion practically on top of one another, and a trillion at the other side of the room.

If space—and technology—permit, the enormous span of time shown here can be underlined with slides. When the first human marker stands in position at one end of the timeline, an image to represent 'today,' perhaps a computer, could be projected behind them. In the middle of the timeline, at 16,000 years ago, an image from the Lascaux Caves in France, and at the far end, 32,000 years ago, an image from the Chauvet caves, also in France. In addition to seeing the difference in the numbers, the audience can see that cave painting constituted a very long art 'movement,' the imagery changing hardly at all during the 16,000 years between Chauvet and Lascaux, compared to art 'isms' of the last two centuries, which have positively tripped along: impressionism, pointillism, fauvism, futurism, cubism, surrealism, etceterism, etceterism.

Up, up and …

In the 'nine ways' chapter, we've seen that it's good to give an audience something they can understand in terms of their own bodies. Here's another example: a stack of one million dollars in $100 bills comes up your waist. Even if you can simply *say* that, people can see it—no graphic is necessary. I know it's an approximation; clearly, there would be more than a million dollars in the stack at Michael Jordan's or LeBron James's waists, while P.T. Barnum's Tom Thumb, who was 3' 4" tall—the same height as the million-dollar stack of $100 bills.

The million-billion-trillion demonstration works best in a wide room; this next one uses a helium balloon to bring a big number down to a human scale, and is best done in a room with a high ceiling. It takes some preparation: I inflated a weather balloon with helium to about 36 inches wide, and used that to raise a 10-foot long string with markers attached to it. Birthday balloons aren't strong enough; they will float up, but they have surprisingly little lifting power if anything is tied onto the string, *(opposite).*

Here's some audience participation without anyone having to come up to the front. (You can try this on Zoom, too.) One, ask everyone to cross their legs. Two, ask them to 'draw' the number 6 in the air in front of them. Three, ask them to rotate the crossed leg in clockwise circles, while also 'drawing' the number 6. People laugh—most can't do it.

What does this exerise have to do with infographics? Nothing. That's the point. What you have done is to have engaged your audience, perhaps even literally made people sit up, and listeners need the occasional break from your intense talk about numbers and zero baselines. Give them a short vacation from your lecture.

One of the best examples of a live 3-d graphic that I've seen is part of the filmed version of David Byrne's *American Utopia,* his theater piece which combines songs with social commentary. During the show, Byrne demonstrates the percentage of people who vote in US state and local elections. He turns the cameras away from the stage to face the audience, and shines a strip of light on 20% of them. The other 80% of the audience is visible, but in shadow.

Fun (and facts) with helium

More evidence that a trillion is a *really* big number.

If a **trillion** is represented by a height of 10 feet (3.048m), a **billion** is just 0.012 inch (0.3048mm) thick.

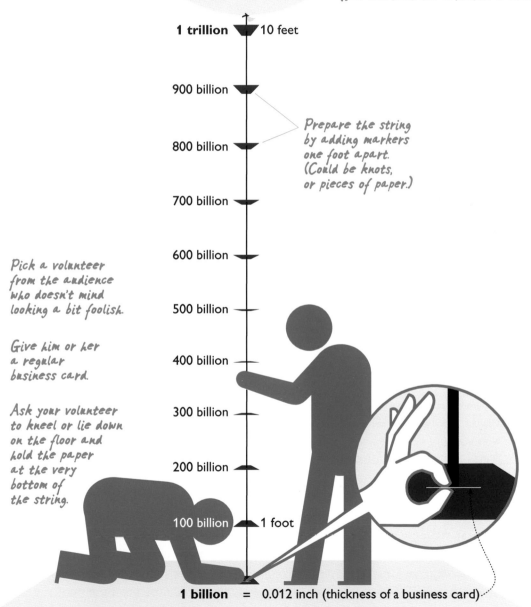

Make sure the ceiling is high enough!

Yes, weather ballons are this big. (At least!)

Fill yours with helium before the presentation. (You can rent small helium tanks.)

1 trillion ▼ 10 feet

900 billion ▼

800 billion ▼

Prepare the string by adding markers one foot apart. (Could be knots, or pieces of paper.)

700 billion ▼

600 billion ▼

Pick a volunteer from the audience who doesn't mind looking a bit foolish.

500 billion ▼

Give him or her a regular business card.

400 billion ▼

300 billion ▼

Ask your volunteer to kneel or lie down on the floor and hold the paper at the very bottom of the string.

200 billion ▼

100 billion ▼ 1 foot

1 billion = 0.012 inch (thickness of a business card)

Byrne's demonstration is a striking example of how few people vote in state and local races. Pointing to the darkened audience he says 'I guess you guys just don't care,' then adds that we all ought to do better in presidential elections, too, when only about 55% of eligible voters bother to go to the polls.

Keep these ideas in mind

You may never intend to involve your audiences in the kind of theatrical things I've attempted, but here are a few things to remember when making presentations.

Plan a beginning and an end to the speech. Famous quotes or sayings can be good openers and enders, but using a joke just for the sake of making people laugh isn't a good idea. *(See John's point above.)*

Use notes, not a script. It's OK to glance down at your notes, but if you have written out your whole speech you'll be looking down all the time, and it's off-putting for the audience. There may be parts of your speech that you do have to read—an important lengthy quote, for instance, that you want to get exactly right—and in that case, pick up your notes so people can see you are reading from them.

Rehearse by yourself, and constantly, while you construct the presentation. The order of your images will affect the words you speak, so do speak them, out loud. I guarantee there will be something you'll want to change.

Rehearse again! Once you have finished compiling the whole presentation, time yourself reading it while you advance the slides. Nothing is more frustrating for you and the organizers than a presenter who goes over the allotted time. Rehearsal will also let you know where you can speed things up in case you get questions during your speech that might make it go longer than you planned.

Use fewer—far fewer—written words on your slides, and think about what you want to get across more as spoken words. (It's called a speech, folks!) The point of a live presentation is that you and your voice are right there in front of people; if you just read your slides, the audience will be confused about whether they should read what's on the screen, or listen to you reading it.

Check the room. Have a look around. If it's a conference with multiple speakers, listen to those who come before you. Reiterating ideas that your fellow speakers have made is not only respectful to them, but it also helps the audience understand both your ideas and others'— even if you disagree. Listening to the presenters before you helps you gauge the overall feeling of the attendees, and if you intend to ask some of them to join you up at the front, you can identify likely candidates from their questions and reactions before it's your time to speak.

Check in early with the audiovisual team (if there is one) to make sure that your computer systems are compatible with the conference's. That way, you'll start on time, and be relaxed about the technology. Preparation is important, especially if you are nervous about public speaking, which most of us are.

Stand up! … next to your computer, not behind it. If the conference is configured with a table and chair for speakers, don't sit there. You will be a much more engaging speaker if you stand and move around the space a bit. And you have arms! Did your parents tell you not to point? This is the time to point! It's like adding a label to an important element in a graphic that you want your audience to take note of. At one of his wonderful presentations, I saw Hans Rosling use the ultimate pointer to interact with his slides—a 10-foot long stick. It was funny, and very effective.

Don't let PowerPoint seduce you into using flashy special effects. I use the program all the time, and I like it, but I only occasionally use its fancy wipes, animations, and 3-d font effects. Just as you should use color sparingly in infographics—color code your graphics to highlight or emphasize information, never use color to decorate them—think of PowerPoint effects in the same way. A deliberate avoidance of special effects however, shouldn't stop you from including animated clips that add information and make presentations lively.

An aside about PowerPoint (or Keynote, or any other presentation program). Many conferences are now virtual, as a result of the Covid pandemic, and presentations are made over Zoom, which is fast becoming the generic name (think Xerox) for all remote meetings. I suspect that when things are back to normal, many conferences will remain virtual, or be a hybrid of in-person and Zoomed-in.

For two reasons, remote presentations are a minefield for lecturers. First, the fact that you can't see the audience is a bigger problem than you might suspect. When you can see the people sitting in front of you, you can see whether or not they understand what you are saying, and you adjust your presentation accordingly. There's an unmistakable connection between a live audience and the speaker—laughs, groans at bad puns, applause, snoring—all feedback that helps and informs the way you talk. During a virtual presentation, you are speaking into a void; your listeners are invisible, muted, and separated from one another.

The second part of the minefield is technology. I'd say that half of all presentations I have either given, or listened to, have included some sort of technical glitch. As I write this, I have just finished remotely presenting at a hybrid conference—part with live presentations in front of an audience, and with my part remotely phoned-in. Despite a rehearsal in advance of the event with the audiovisual technicians, two-thirds of the way through my session half of my screen was inexplicably covered with an irrelevant file. Neither the technical team nor anyone in the audience was able to help me; I could hear people shouting contradictory suggestions.

After a few flailing minutes, the meeting host wisely shut me down.

The moral: you can never do too much planning for the technical part of a presentation. And in the same way that I make friends with the AV people at in-person lectures, you should try to contact remote digital helpers, and tell them about any problems you may have had with previous events. Perhaps more importantly, if you are in the Apple camp, as I am, find out if they are as conversant with Apple products as they are with PCs. AV people seem to be mostly in the latter camp, at least at digital conferences.

Handouts. The idea that slides can have a dual purpose—to be both the presentation and also a leave-behind—is wrong. It's more work to make a separate document that you can leave behind, tailored to a reader (instead of a listener/viewer), but it makes sense. Use both mediums—your live presentation and a written leave-behind document—to their best advantage; they are not interchangeable. This is the graphic handout I left behind after the million, billion, trillion presentation.

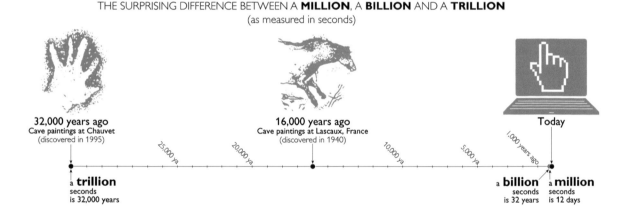

THE SURPRISING DIFFERENCE BETWEEN A **MILLION**, A **BILLION** AND A **TRILLION**
(as measured in seconds)

32,000 years ago
Cave paintings at Chauvet
(discovered in 1995)

16,000 years ago
Cave paintings at Lascaux, France
(discovered in 1940)

Today

25,000 ya   20,000 ya   10,000 ya   5,000 ya   1,000 years ago

a **trillion**
seconds
is 32,000 years

a **billion**
seconds
is 32 years

a **million**
seconds
is 12 days

'The End' … is better wording for your last slide; it's more direct, a bit funny, and less abrupt than 'Questions?' And please thank your audience in person—say it out loud—rather than writing it on a slide. It's much friendlier.

Next: Science graphics.

breathe

Science: serious fun

Scientists are serious people. They don't want their work to be trivialized by graphic designers. I understand. For a diagram running in *Time* about interferons—proteins that induce resistance to viral infections in nearby cells—we sent the finished piece to the scientist who was featured in the article. He was horrified that his life's work was going to be illustrated with a comic strip, and in *Time* magazine, no less.

Interferons are messenger RNA, so I had drawn Paul Revere riding from one cell to another, warning the second cell that a virus was coming, and that it should put up a defense.

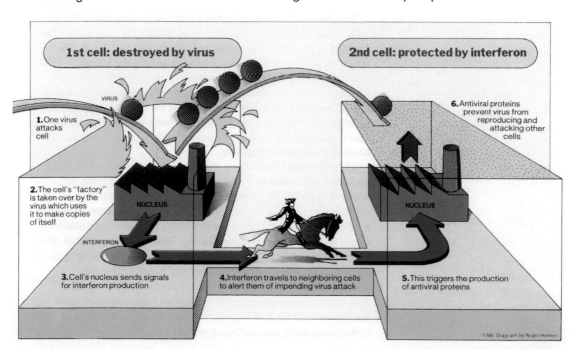

We published the graphic *(above)* anyway, since the scientist could find nothing wrong with the facts, however much he objected to the way they were presented. After the magazine came out, he got letters from his colleagues saying in effect 'now we understand your work,' and he generously told us. (We got letters like that from readers, too.)

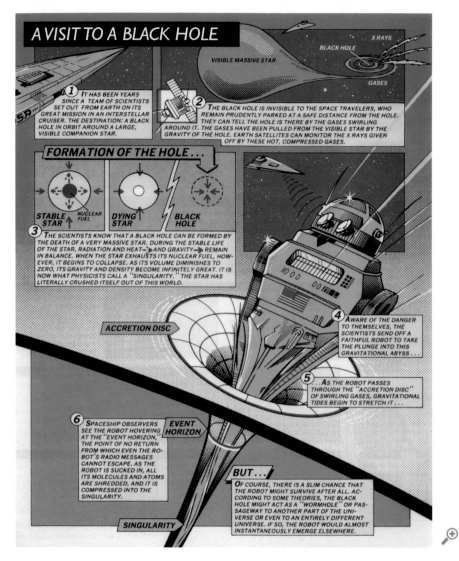

So what if it looked like a comic? *Time's* Art Director Walter Bernard allowed me to mess with the magazine's page design and draw an real comic for a graphic about black holes *(above)*. The juxtaposition of a freewheeling comic-book style with *Time's* restrained and gridded structure made the piece all the more—dare I say it—joyful.

Years later, Jen Christiansen, graphics director at Scientific American, contacted me about another black hole story. I asked her to tell me about that commission:
'*When I read the preliminary draft of an article by Adam Brown for the February 2015 issue of Scientific American, Nigel Holmes popped immediately to my mind as a great artist for the project. The title "Can We Mine a Black Hole?" sounded straightforward enough: Intriguing, and presumably on the technical and expository end of things. A title like that suggests that complex physics diagrams or equations may follow. But the deck—a few lines of display text directly below the headline—*

opened the door to whimsy. "Let's say some future civilization wanted to get energy out of a black hole. The first step would be to build a space elevator that defies the laws of physics."

'I wanted graphics that would match the tone of the deck. An imprecise and playful vibe would reinforce that the article was centered on a thought experiment. We weren't showing objects that were currently being built and tested. I was after something more in the spirit of scientists jotting down ideas and doodling in a notebook while thinking through the hypothetical possibilities. Nigel's illustrations, (right), provided an informal and welcoming gesture to non-scientist and scientist readers alike, thanks to his content choices and style.'

I don't know if Jen ever saw the *Time* comic, but she told me she had seen two more recent graphics that made her think of me for her black hole assignment. One was for *The New York Times*, a series of hand-drawn illustrations about the Higgs boson, and the other a collaboration with the theoretical physicist Michio Kaku for the 100th anniversary of Einstein's Special Theory of Relativity in *Discover* magazine. (See one of the spreads on the next page.)

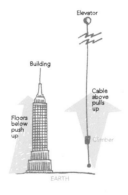

Some of the art for The New York Times' Higgs boson story, describing the Higgs field first like molasses and then using a metaphor of a field of snow. On the Times website, the whole sequence of 20 drawings were beautifully animated by Xaquín G.V.

Special Relativity

Special relativity unlocked the secret of the stars and revealed the untold energy stored deep inside the atom. But the seed of relativity was planted when Einstein was only 16 years old, when he asked himself a children's question: what would a beam of light look like if you could race along side?

   According to Newton, you could catch up to any speeding object if you moved fast enough. Catching up to a light wave, it would look like a wave frozen in time. But even as a child, Einstein knew that no one had ever seen a frozen wave before.

   When Einstein studied Maxwell's theory of light, he found something that others missed, that the speed of light was always constant, no matter how fast you moved. He then boldly formulated the principle of special relativity: the speed of light is a constant in all inertial frames (frames which move at constant velocity).

   No longer were space and time absolutes, as Newton thought. Clocks beat at different rates throughout the universe. This is a profound departure from the Newtonian world.

Previously, physicists believed in the "ether," a mysterious substance which pervaded the universe and provided the absolute reference frame for all motions. But the Michelson-Morely experiment measured the "ether wind" of the earth as it moved around the sun, and it was zero. Either the earth was motionless, or the meter sticks in the experiment had somehow shortened. In desperation to save Newtonian physics, some believed that the atoms in meter sticks were mechanically compressed by the force of the ether wind. Einstein showed that the ether theory was totally unnecessary, that space itself contracted and time slowed down as you moved near the speed of light...

→ 186,282 miles per second

Imagine a policeman on a motorcycle catching up to a speeding motorist.

According to Newton, the policeman would see the driver as if he were at rest.

But if we watch this from the sidewalk, we'd see the policeman and the driver racing past neck and neck.

Now replace the motorist with a light beam.

From the sidewalk, we see the policeman racing right alongside the light beam. But later, if you talked to the policeman, he would shake his head and say that no matter how fast he accelerated, the light beam raced ahead at the speed of light, leaving him in the dust.

But how can the policeman's story differ so much from what we just saw from the sidewalk with our own eyes? Einstein was stunned when he found the answer: time itself had slowed down for everything on the policeman's motorcycle.

To Newton, time was uniform throughout the universe. One second on Mars was the same as one second on earth. One o'clock on earth was the same as one o'clock on Mars.

But to Einstein, time beats at different rates. The faster you travel, the slower time beats. There is no such thing as absolute time. When you say that it is one o'clock on earth, it's not necessarily one o'clock throughout the universe.

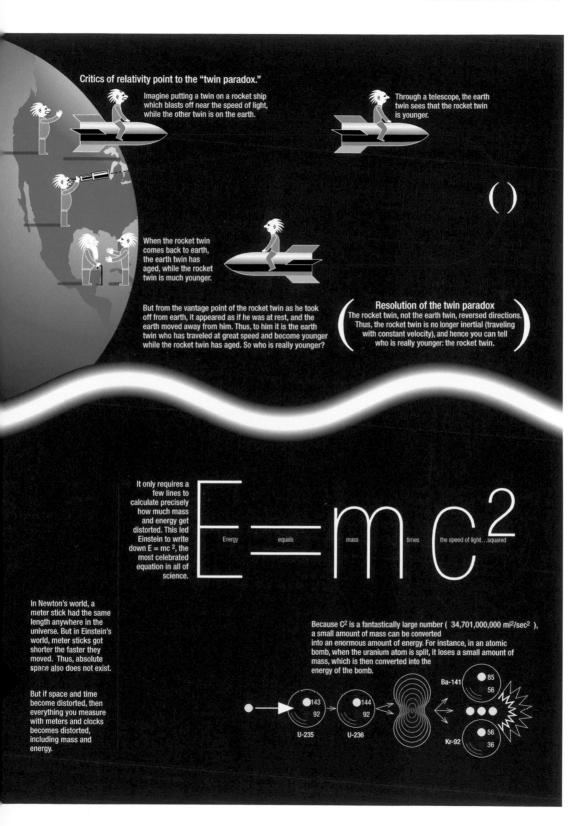

Critics of relativity point to the "twin paradox."

Imagine putting a twin on a rocket ship which blasts off near the speed of light, while the other twin is on the earth.

Through a telescope, the earth twin sees that the rocket twin is younger.

When the rocket twin comes back to earth, the earth twin has aged, while the rocket twin is much younger.

But from the vantage point of the rocket twin as he took off from earth, it appeared as if he was at rest, and the earth moved away from him. Thus, to him it is the earth twin who has traveled at great speed and become younger while the rocket twin has aged. So who is really younger?

Resolution of the twin paradox
The rocket twin, not the earth twin, reversed directions. Thus, the rocket twin is no longer inertial (traveling with constant velocity), and hence you can tell who is really younger: the rocket twin.

It only requires a few lines to calculate precisely how much mass and energy get distorted. This led Einstein to write down $E = mc^2$, the most celebrated equation in all of science.

$$E = mc^2$$

Energy   equals   mass   times   the speed of light...squared

In Newton's world, a meter stick had the same length anywhere in the universe. But in Einstein's world, meter sticks got shorter the faster they moved. Thus, absolute space also does not exist.

But if space and time become distorted, then everything you measure with meters and clocks becomes distorted, including mass and energy.

Because C^2 is a fantastically large number (34,701,000,000 mi²/sec²), a small amount of mass can be converted into an enormous amount of energy. For instance, in an atomic bomb, when the uranium atom is split, it loses a small amount of mass, which is then converted into the energy of the bomb.

U-235   U-236

Ba-141   85
56

56
Kr-92   36

Design Director Michael Mrak and editors Stephen Petranek and David Grogan thought that a collaborative effort—text and pictures welded together—rather than a long article illustrated with diagrams, would be good way to celebrate Einstein. And it would be an interesting change of pace for the magaine. It was a delight working with Michio, who willingly gave up a much easier job for him—writing a 4,000-word article—and instead engaged with a designer who knew next to nothing about his subject. After lots of back-and-forth between us, he selflessly ended up writing what amounted to extended captions for my graphics, *(previous spread)*.

Working directly with scientists who really know their stuff, and who are able to stand back and look at it from the point of view of a reader who probably doesn't know anything about

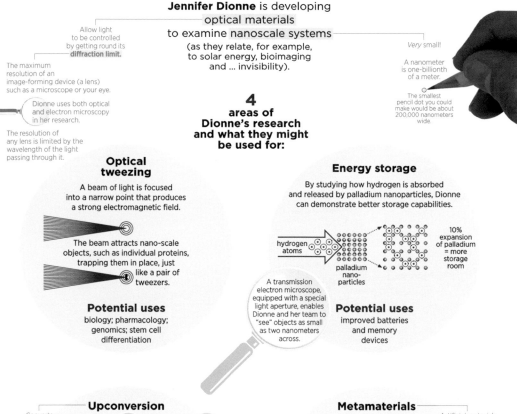

Jennifer Dionne is developing optical materials to examine nanoscale systems (as they relate, for example, to solar energy, bioimaging and … invisibility).

Allow light to be controlled by getting round its **diffraction limit.**

The maximum resolution of an image-forming device (a lens) such as a microscope or your eye.

Dionne uses both optical and electron microscopy in her research.

The resolution of any lens is limited by the wavelength of the light passing through it.

Very small!

A nanometer is one-billionth of a meter.

The smallest pencil dot you could make would be about 200,000 nanometers wide.

4 areas of Dionne's research and what they might be used for:

Optical tweezing

A beam of light is focused into a narrow point that produces a strong electromagnetic field.

The beam attracts nano-scale objects, such as individual proteins, trapping them in place, just like a pair of tweezers.

Potential uses
biology; pharmacology; genomics; stem cell differentiation

Energy storage

By studying how hydrogen is absorbed and released by palladium nanoparticles, Dionne can demonstrate better storage capabilities.

hydrogen atoms

palladium nano-particles

10% expansion of palladium = more storage room

A transmission electron microscope, equipped with a special light aperture, enables Dionne and her team to "see" objects as small as two nanometers across.

Potential uses
improved batteries and memory devices

Upconversion

Converts low-energy photons to higher-energy photons

solar panel

30%–50% of incoming rays are not absorbed …

… adding an insulator and an upconverter increases absorption

Potential uses
more efficient, carbon-neutral solar panels; hi-res visualization of biological forces and fields in neuronal actions of the brain and spine

Metamaterials

Artificial materials with properties not yet found in nature

positive (ordinary) refraction

negative refraction in liquid metamaterial

The tiny structures in these new materials are smaller than the wavelength of light. When properly constructed, metamaterials guide rays of light around objects, allowing a surgeon, for instance, to operate without seeing his own hands.

Potential uses
optical microscope lenses that can potentially "see" DNA; ultra-compact zoom lenses for cameras; nanoscale optical transistors

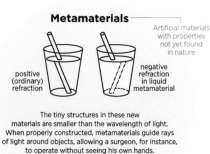
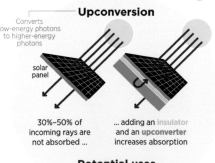

it, is a gift to infographic designers. Jennifer Dionne, a scientist at Stanford University, was to be featured in *Stanford* magazine for her work on nanoscale systems. Stanford alumni are probably the smartest readers a designer will come across, meaning that they might not need much help understanding Jennifer's experiments. Still, I couldn't resist trying to explain how very small nanoparticles are. As printed in the magazine the hand in the diagram *(left)* is life size, so the reader can put their own hand right there. It gives a general idea of the size of a nanometer but doesn't quite work; as the text guiltily notes, the dot made by the pencil is still 500,000 times too large! For the rest of the graphic I tried, with Jennifer's helpful editing, to make her complicated work available to laypeople—even if they were smart!

Explaining science to children

You know, it isn't that different from explaining science to non-children—sometimes called adults. (Although 'adult' is more about age than intelligence or attitude; I'm just an older child.)

Considering our audience of children—and 'older' children—in this way is good because a fundamental explanation of anything should go back to the basics of any subject; it should assume no prior knowledge. Graphics aimed at children might look brighter and more jolly than stuff made for an adult audience, but the facts should always be clear. Several infographical people have had a go: *I am a book. I am a portal to the universe by* designer Stefanie Posavec and data journalist Miriam Quick is a clever kaleidoscope of images and words about what Planet Earth is made of, and how a book—the actual book that you are holding while you read it—relates to all the science described. In the small print at the back, Stefanie and Miriam detail the math and science behind the concepts they have so brilliantly and simply illustrated.

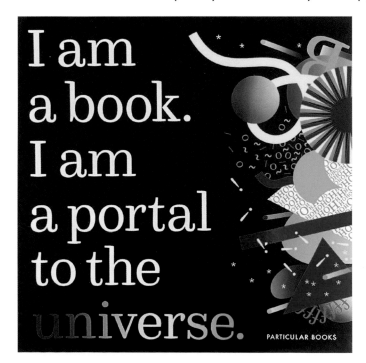

Simon Rogers, the data editor at Google, has written a great series of books for children, collaborating with illustrators and infographic designers—Peter Grundy on the *Human Body*; Jennifer Daniel, *Space!*; Nicholas Blechman, *Animal Kingdom*; Studio Muti, *Technology*.

A much earlier information-filled series for children was written and illustrated by Holling Clancy Holling. Along with an adventure story (including *Tree in the Trail,* 1942, and *Seabird,* 1948), that is straightforwardly told in text, Holling fills his pages with realistic full-color paintings of the action, and black-and-white charts, maps and diagrams in the margins that explain everything from Indian canoe-making, to how river locks, volcanoes, and covered wagons work; how to read tree rings; and the biology of embryonic cell division. The books are science, art and adventure all in one package.

Marie Neurath continued the work of her husband Otto's *Isotype* Institute after his death in 1945. As well as doing ground-breaking graphic work in Africa, Marie created books for children that explained aspects of science, and how people lived in the past. *The Visual History of Mankind, Wonders of the Modern World, The Wonder World of Nature* and other series, produced until the early 1970s, used the same visual principles of clarity and color-coding that Otto and his team had advocated from the start of the Vienna Method.

This is a not at all a comprehensive list of books about science for children; they are the ones I admire. Each has lessons for information designers about how to explain ideas in a clear manner. All are beautifully designed and are well worth reading for the fun and for the lessons.

I've written two books for children. They are stories with lots of explanatory diagrams. The first one is about *Pinhole*, a tiny person—almost invisible (an arrow shows you where he is). In one adventure, Pinhole goes for a ride on the back of a insect, *(below).*

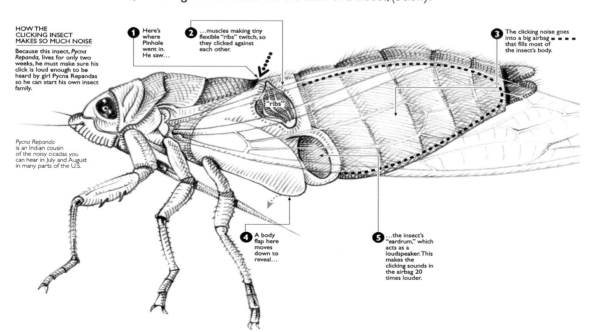

HOW THE CLICKING INSECT MAKES SO MUCH NOISE

Because this insect, *Pycna Repanda,* lives for only two weeks, he must make sure his click is loud enough to be heard by girl Pycna Repandas so he can start his own insect family.

Pycna Repanda is an Indian cousin of the noisy cicadas you can hear in July and August in many parts of the U.S.

1 Here's where Pinhole went in. He saw...

2 ...muscles making tiny flexible "ribs" twitch, so they clicked against each other.

"ribs"

3 The clicking noise goes into a big airbag that fills most of the insect's body.

4 A body flap here moves down to reveal...

5 ...the insect's "eardrum," which acts as a loudspeaker. This makes the clicking sounds in the airbag 20 times louder.

In one chapter of *Art Blob*, the title character *(below)* makes cheese (it doesn't turn out well).

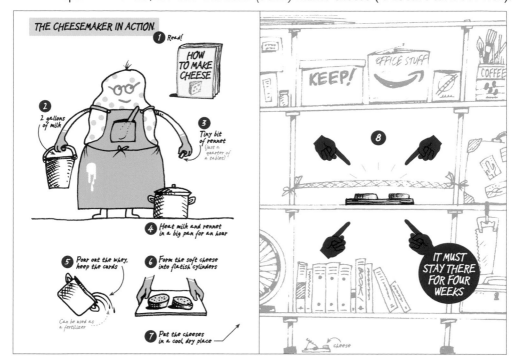

An edible infographic As part of a course for professional infographic designers that ran from 1984 to 1993 at the Rhode Island School of Design, one exercise was to devise a way to explain a difficult subject to a child, in front of the class. There was no limit to how this could be done: any way the explanation was presented was fair game. It brought out the theatrical side of the students, and provided a relief from intense chart- and map-making; and it broadened the idea of what an infographic could be. My favorite piece was an explanation of why a child's mother would need special care and attention when she came home from the hospital after an operation to fix a slipped disc. The students, one playing the father, and one the child, made a model of a spine out of a hot dog, donuts and cheese slices. Since the construction was flexible, you could see how a piece of cheese, standing in for the errant disc, was awkwardly squeezed between two donut-vertebrae, causing pain. Everyone laughed, but we got the point. Naturally, the 'father and child' finished their presentation by eating the whole thing.

The science of laughing and smiling.

Before I attempt to explain this, two caveats: (1) I am not a scientist, and (2) My wife groans at my jokes—but then sometimes laughs because they are *so* bad. When I'm away from home making a presentation, I often give the audience a card, *(left),* to hold up to their face. I would then take a photo of the assembled group and email it home to let Erin know that at least the audience thought I was funny.

On the back of the card there was a brief explanation of why smiling is good for you. The first graphic on the back of the card was the Smile-o-graph©, but it wasn't that funny. Who needs a joke when there's plenty of *real* science about laughter and smiling, and jokes?

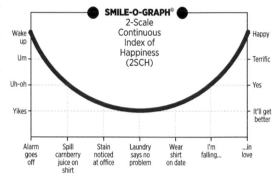

For instance, Scott Weems' revealing and hilarious book *Ha! The Science of When We Laugh and Why* goes into great detail about how a region in the front of the brain—the anterior cingulate—monitors our responses to humor, particularly jokes. And the psychologist Richard Wiseman has written extensively about jokes; in 2001, he started a quest to find the world's funniest. 40,000 jokes were sent in to his project website, *LaughLab*. They were rated by more than 350,000 people from 70 countries, and a winner was proclaimed.

Five years after that study, Wiseman found a slightly different version of the winning joke that was written by Spike Milligan in the 1950s and was first told on the radio by two members of the *Goon Show*—those funny people cited among my early influences. This is Milligan's version of the World's Funniest Joke:

> *Michael Bentine: I just came in and found him lying on the carpet there.*
> *Peter Sellers: Oh, is he dead?*
> *Bentine: I think so.*
> *Sellers: Hadn't you better make sure?*
> *Bentine: Alright. Just a minute.*
> *Sound of two gunshots.*
> *Bentine: He's dead.*—transcribed from Richard Wiseman's blog.

(Yes, I had the same reaction: *that's* the World's Funniest Joke?)

This book isn't about jokes, and why you 'get' them, or don't. What interests me is the kind of good feeling that flows over you when you smile. All sorts of experts from 'happiness gurus' to a TED talker have weighed in on the benefits of smiling.

This is my take on the complexity of the simple act of smiling.

First, the mechanical part. We have more than 30 facial muscles that pull the face into different expressions. When we smile, our *zygomaticus* muscles (major and minor), and our *risorius* muscles are triggered by a neurotransmitter, acetylcholine, that pulls the mouth up and back, while our *orbicularis oculi* muscles narrow our eyes. While we can control the *zygomaticus* and *risorius* muscles, we cannot activate the *orbicularis oculi* at will, and if we try to, it leads to an insincere, or fake smile. In 1862, Guillaume-Benjamin Duchenne de Boulogne demonstrated this difference between a 'real' smile, when the mouth is tugged up and the eyes are narrowed —the *Duchenne* Smile—and a 'fake' smile, when we force a grin (a *non-Duchenne* smile).

Second, the chemical part. When we smile, the brain releases three hormones: dopamine, endorphins, and serotonin. Dopamine, known as the feel-good, and 'reward' neurotransmitter, is a chemical messenger which is released from the hypothalamus during pleasurable situations. Endorphins, released by the pituitary gland, are morphine-like chemicals that produce euphoria. Serotonin is an anti-depressant and stress reducer responsible for feelings of satisfaction and contentment.

Are there too many obscure medical terms here? Seems like the perfect place for me to shut up and draw you a friendly diagram—it's a more science-y version of the card I handed out when speaking at conferences.

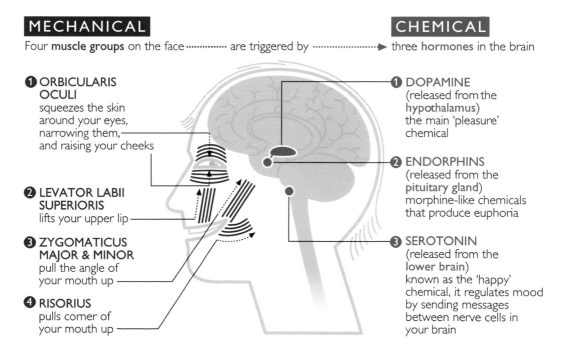

MECHANICAL

Four **muscle groups** on the face ·············· are triggered by ····················▶

❶ ORBICULARIS OCULI
squeezes the skin around your eyes, narrowing them, and raising your cheeks

❷ LEVATOR LABII SUPERIORIS
lifts your upper lip

❸ ZYGOMATICUS MAJOR & MINOR
pull the angle of your mouth up

❹ RISORIUS
pulls corner of your mouth up

CHEMICAL

three **hormones** in the brain

❶ DOPAMINE
(released from the hypothalamus)
the main 'pleasure' chemical

❷ ENDORPHINS
(released from the pituitary gland)
morphine-like chemicals that produce euphoria

❸ SEROTONIN
(released from the lower brain)
known as the 'happy' chemical, it regulates mood by sending messages between nerve cells in your brain

By the way, to make serotonin, you need tryptophan—an essential bio-chemical precursor—and a great place to get it is from cheese. That's why those of us who love cheese cannot get enough of it—we are addicted. It goes like this:

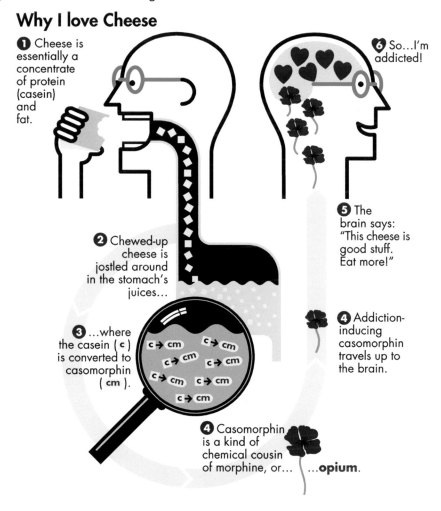

Why I love Cheese

1 Cheese is essentially a concentrate of protein (casein) and fat.

2 Chewed-up cheese is jostled around in the stomach's juices...

3 ...where the casein (c) is converted to casomorphin (cm).

4 Casomorphin is a kind of chemical cousin of morphine, or... ...**opium**.

4 Addiction-inducing casomorphin travels up to the brain.

5 The brain says: "This cheese is good stuff. Eat more!"

6 So...I'm addicted!

All the smiling muscle stuff can be stopped cold by injecting Botox into the faces of people hoping to appear ageless. Botox freezes the muscles so your wrinkles don't deepen over time. It's a neurotoxin that attaches itself to nerve endings, and when it does, acetylcholine—which normally triggers muscle contractions—doesn't work. In extreme cases, you can't smile. You can't frown either. Some patients are happy with that; it makes them appear happier.

Scientists who study these things say that our brains can be tricked into thinking that humor is present by forcing a smile—that *non-Duchenne* Smile—assuming our ability to smile at all hasn't been botoxed away. Apparently, muscle movement by itself can trigger the release of happiness hormones. It follows that when we obey a photographer's 'smile, please,' at least we'll feel good when the camera clicks, even if we feel a bit silly doing it.

Smiling is contagious, like yawning. It's the work of *mirror neurons* in the brain which fire when we see someone yawn…

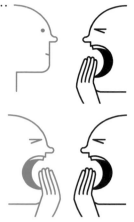

… or smile.

Perhaps that's why Danish-American comedian Victor Borge said
'A smile is the shortest distance between people.'

A fitting end to this science lecture.

Next pages: a collection of sciency graphics from magazines, books, and newspapers.

Space

Putting an Arm on Space

Columbia *is back with upside-down experiments*

Nothing quite like it has ever been attempted in space. As the gleaming white-and-black orbiter hurtles across the skies, a long, mechanical arm, rather like the boom of a cherry picker, will emerge slowly from the spacecraft's cargo bay. Bending and flexing its metallic muscles, the multijointed limb will reach out into space almost as if it were guided by an independent intelligence of its own.

The high-level arm-twisting should be the highlight of the space shuttle *Columbia's* second flight, slated to begin with another thunderous Florida lift-off at 7:30 a.m., E.S.T., this Wednesday.

When the shuttle made its first flight last April, NASA sought to prove to itself and the world that the craft could really roar up into space like a rocket, then glide safely back to earth like a plane. This week the U.S. space agency is engaging in quite another sort of test. Flying "upside down" high above the earth, *Columbia* will try out a $100 million, Canadian-built "arm in space." Unless the Remote Manipulator System, as the huge skyhook is called in NASA jargon, really works, the shuttle will be unable to perform one of its key roles in space: to place satellites into orbit and retrieve them when they fail.

NASA's unsurprising name for the second test of its Space Transportation System is S.T.S.-2. *Columbia* will be piloted by a new crew, Air Force Colonel Joe H. Engle, 49, the lean, affable mission commander who likes to hunt bear with bow and arrow, and Navy Captain Richard H. Truly, 43. Both are veteran pilots who began training as astronauts in the 1960s but who only

now will be making orbital flights. The shuttle will be packed with more fuel and equipment than it was last April, including seven experiments, and it is slated to stay aloft at least five days instead of only two. After 83 complete orbits of the earth, if all goes according to plan, Engle will pilot the orbiter to another dead-stick landing on the dusty, dried-out old lake bed of California's Edwards Air Force Base. Estimated touchdown time: shortly after noon, Eastern time, next Monday, Nov. 9.

For a while it looked like the second flight might never get off the pad. Miscalculations and errors caused repeated delays. In the first flight an unexpectedly powerful shock wave from the initial blast of the shuttle's solid-fuel rockets caused the control flaps on the trailing edge of *Columbia's* delta wings to flutter so wildly that they approached the breaking point. The shock also bent and buckled several of the metal trusses linking *Columbia* to its big external fuel tank. To prevent a recurrence of this near disaster, engineers had to undertake a complete

overhaul of the shock-suppression system, deluging the flame pits on the launch pad beneath *Columbia's* solid-fuel rockets with even more water.

Still another costly delay followed a mishap on the pad that occurred during a supposedly routine fueling operation when a jammed valve caused a back-up of nitrogen tetroxide. The corrosive liquid, which was part of the mix that powers 14 small maneuvering rockets on *Columbia's* nose, spilled down the orbiter's sides, loosening some 50 of the craft's 31,000 heat-shielding tiles and damaging others. In all, 379 tiles had to be detached, cleaned and reglued. One consequence of these nagging mishaps: NASA officials no longer talk of refurbishing, refueling and sending the shuttle back into orbit every two weeks, and have cut the number of flights over the next four years from 44 to only 32.

After reaching an altitude of 158 miles, the astronauts will open the shuttle's big cargo-bay doors, power up their experiments and conduct the usual checkout of the shuttle's systems. Using its maneuvering rockets, *Columbia* will be rolled over, so that the instruments in the cargo

MISSION OBJECTIVES
Testing remote arm

Cabin experiments
1. Filming lightning during thunderstorms on earth
2. Zero-gravity plant growth

TV monitors

Shoulder joints

Cargo bay
Spacelab pallet
Upper arm

Elbow joint
Elbow TV

Lower arm

Cargo bay experiments
1. Classifying terrain to be studied
2. Mapping geological features
3. Searching for minerals
4. Measuring air pollution
5. Mapping fish and algae distribution

TIME Diagram by Nigel Holmes

Wrist joints
Wrist TV and light

End effector (hand)

Wires close around and grip handle attached to satellite

Handle

Earth

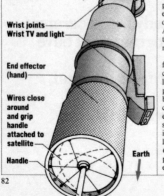

When I showed my sketches for this graphic to editors at Time, they turned it round, assuming I'd handed it to them upside down. They had their way in the end, anyway, writing a subhead to make sure readers didn't think the magazine had made a mistake. The piece was created in 1981, before we had computers in the art department, and it's a testament to the careful work of Time's layout artists, who had to measure and specify all those line-lengths around the mechanical arm, by hand.

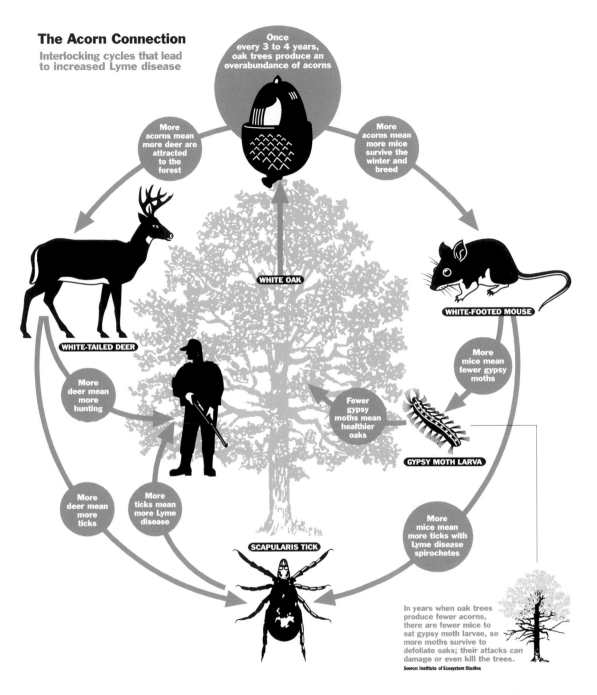

The Acorn Connection
Interlocking cycles that lead to increased Lyme disease

Once every 3 to 4 years, oak trees produce an overabundance of acorns

More acorns mean more deer are attracted to the forest

More acorns mean more mice survive the winter and breed

WHITE OAK

WHITE-FOOTED MOUSE

WHITE-TAILED DEER

More mice mean fewer gypsy moths

More deer mean more hunting

Fewer gypsy moths mean healthier oaks

GYPSY MOTH LARVA

More deer mean more ticks

More ticks mean more Lyme disease

More mice mean more ticks with Lyme disease spirochetes

SCAPULARIS TICK

In years when oak trees produce fewer acorns, there are fewer mice to eat gypsy moth larvae, so more moths survive to defoliate oaks; their attacks can damage or even kill the trees.
Source: Institute of Ecosystem Studies

I live in Connecticut, the state that includes Lyme, the small coastal town where the disease was first identified. I've had it twice, so I was happy to find out more about how it gets passed on, doing this graphic for The New York Times, in 1996.

HOW CAFFEINE WORKS

Caffeine has a molecular structure similar to **adenosine**, a chemical messenger that flows from cell to cell in the brain **slowing cerebral activity** and regulating sleep and wakefulness.

This molecular similarity between caffeine and adenosine allows caffeine to "pose" as adenosine and "fit" into the receptors on brain cells, effectively blocking the adenosine. But the effects of caffeine are very different from those of adenosine. Instead of calming the brain, **caffeine speeds up activity**, helping you to concentrate and fight fatigue.

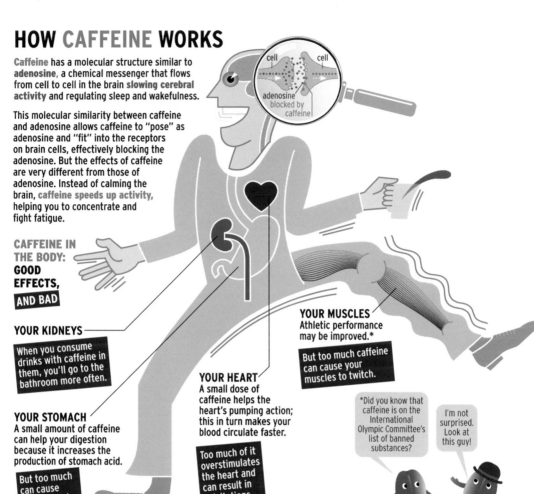

CAFFEINE IN THE BODY: GOOD EFFECTS, AND BAD

cell cell
adenosine blocked by caffeine

YOUR KIDNEYS

When you consume drinks with caffeine in them, you'll go to the bathroom more often.

YOUR STOMACH
A small amount of caffeine can help your digestion because it increases the production of stomach acid.

But too much can cause stomach pains and nausea.

YOUR HEART
A small dose of caffeine helps the heart's pumping action; this in turn makes your blood circulate faster.

Too much of it overstimulates the heart and can result in palpitations.

YOUR MUSCLES
Athletic performance may be improved.*

But too much caffeine can cause your muscles to twitch.

*Did you know that caffeine is on the International Olympic Committee's list of banned substances?

I'm not surprised. Look at this guy!

You've already seen several graphics that first appeared in the 'How It Works' section of Attaché, the in-flight magazine of USAir (later, US Airways; later still, merged with American Airlines). As bored (or nervous) travelers flipped through the stuff in the seat pocket in front of them, we tried to hold their attention for a few minutes with fun facts.

The graphic above from 2002, and seven on the following pages are all from that monthly commission, too. Writer Jim Collins sent me his text weeks before publication so that I could either expand on his ideas, or add my own, but never just parrot what he was saying. Art Director Holly Holliday allowed me almost complete freedom. A dream job!

The graphics were often tied to the time of the year (for instance, Fall, bottom right); or to an event in the news—the release of new US currency designs (top right).

Many of the graphics included the idea of a 'Greek chorus' of characters, commenting on, or making a joke about the piece.

HOW TO TELL IF IT'S FORGED

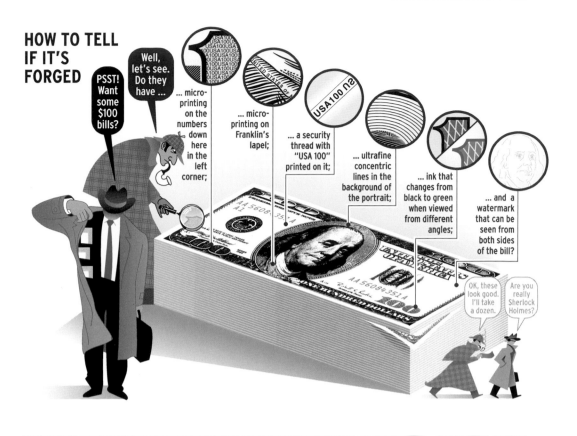

NATURE'S ART

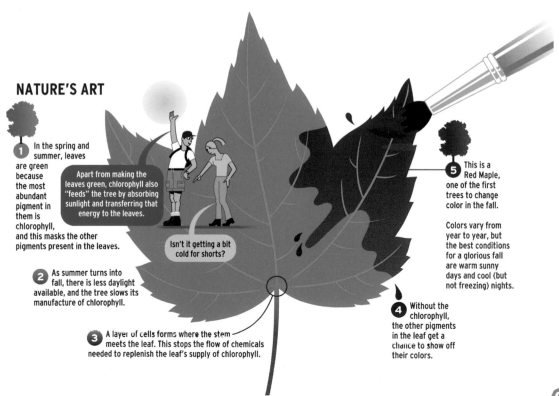

HOW ARTHROSCOPIC SURGERY CAN MEND A TORN CARTILAGE
(Surgeons call it the meniscus.)

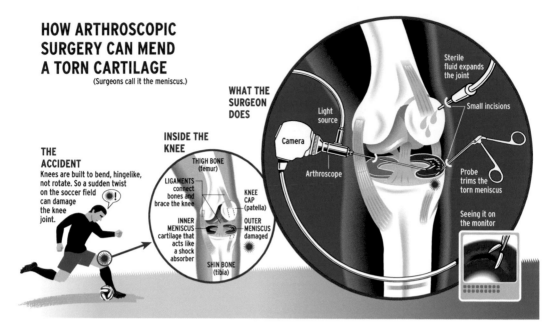

Above and below,
from Attaché, 1999.

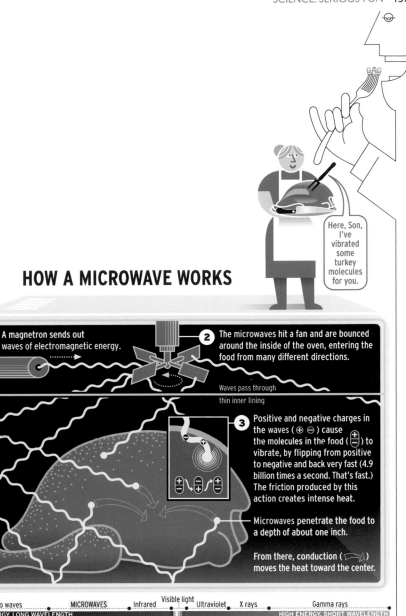

HOW A MICROWAVE WORKS

Here, Son, I've vibrated some turkey molecules for you.

1 A magnetron sends out waves of electromagnetic energy.

2 The microwaves hit a fan and are bounced around the inside of the oven, entering the food from many different directions.

Waves pass through thin inner lining

3 Positive and negative charges in the waves (⊕ ⊖) cause the molecules in the food ( ) to vibrate, by flipping from positive to negative and back very fast (4.9 billion times a second. That's fast.) The friction produced by this action creates intense heat.

Microwaves penetrate the food to a depth of about one inch.

From there, conduction ( ) moves the heat toward the center.

Don't worry too much about radiation—microwaves are down here at the safer end of the spectrum.

Radio waves · MICROWAVES · Infrared · Visible light · Ultraviolet · X rays · Gamma rays

LOW ENERGY, LONG WAVELENGTH   HIGH ENERGY, SHORT WAVELENGTH

From Attaché, 1998. Occasionally I played with the graphic architecture of the page; here, the right-hand page rule becomes a human part of the illustration.

From Attaché, 2002. Like the microwave graphic, this one also gets the right-hand page-rule in on the action, this time as a piano string.

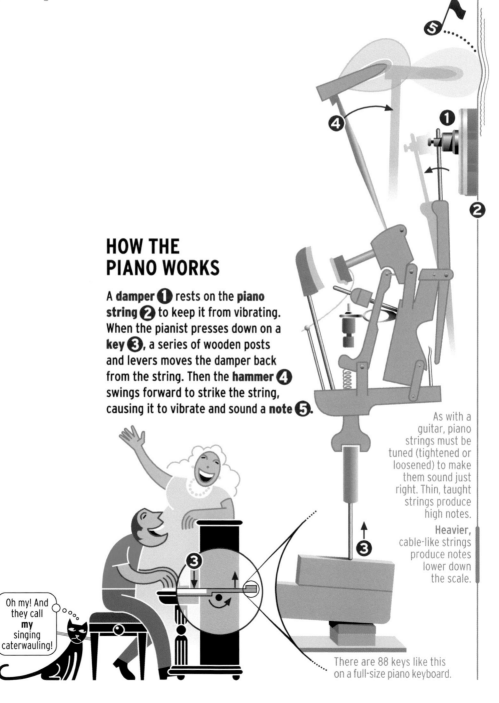

HOW THE PIANO WORKS

A **damper** ❶ rests on the **piano string** ❷ to keep it from vibrating. When the pianist presses down on a **key** ❸, a series of wooden posts and levers moves the damper back from the string. Then the **hammer** ❹ swings forward to strike the string, causing it to vibrate and sound a **note** ❺.

As with a guitar, piano strings must be tuned (tightened or loosened) to make them sound just right. Thin, taught strings produce high notes.

Heavier, cable-like strings produce notes lower down the scale.

There are 88 keys like this on a full-size piano keyboard.

Oh my! And they call **my** singing caterwauling!

METABOLISM: YOUR FOOD PROCESSOR

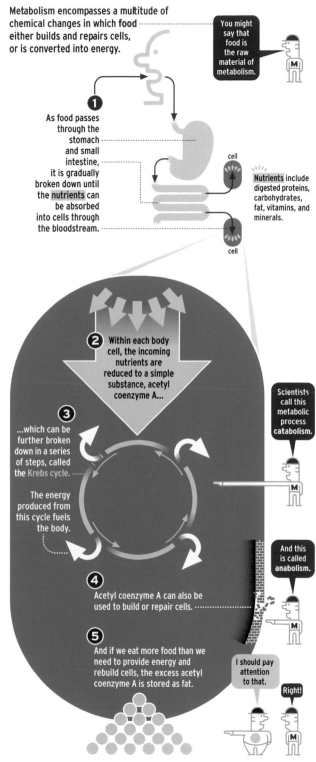

Metabolism encompasses a multitude of chemical changes in which food either builds and repairs cells, or is converted into energy.

You might say that food is the raw material of metabolism.

1 As food passes through the stomach and small intestine, it is gradually broken down until the nutrients can be absorbed into cells through the bloodstream.

cell

Nutrients include digested proteins, carbohydrates, fat, vitamins, and minerals.

cell

2 Within each body cell, the incoming nutrients are reduced to a simple substance, acetyl coenzyme A...

Scientists call this metabolic process catabolism.

3 ...which can be further broken down in a series of steps, called the Krebs cycle.

The energy produced from this cycle fuels the body.

And this is called anabolism.

4 Acetyl coenzyme A can also be used to build or repair cells.

5 And if we eat more food than we need to provide energy and rebuild cells, the excess acetyl coenzyme A is stored as fat.

I should pay attention to that.

Right!

From Attaché, 2004. In this one, the 'little people' are adding to, and explaining the information more than just making comments.

AN EYE FOR AN EYE

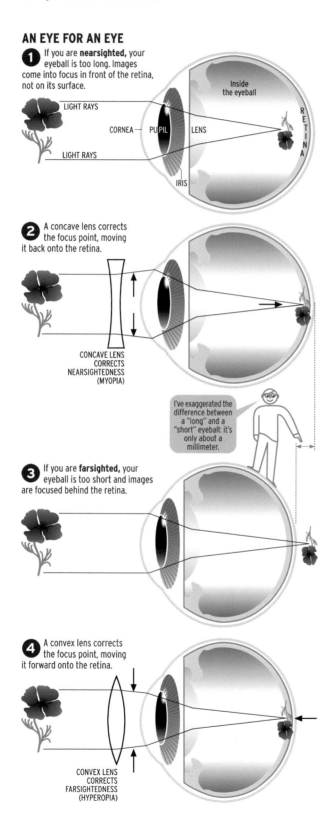

1 If you are **nearsighted**, your eyeball is too long. Images come into focus in front of the retina, not on its surface.

LIGHT RAYS

CORNEA — PUPIL   LENS

Inside the eyeball

R E T I N A

LIGHT RAYS

IRIS

2 A concave lens corrects the focus point, moving it back onto the retina.

CONCAVE LENS CORRECTS NEARSIGHTEDNESS (MYOPIA)

I've exaggerated the difference between a "long" and a "short" eyeball: it's only about a millimeter.

3 If you are **farsighted**, your eyeball is too short and images are focused behind the retina.

4 A convex lens corrects the focus point, moving it forward onto the retina.

CONVEX LENS CORRECTS FARSIGHTEDNESS (HYPEROPIA)

From Attaché, 2005.
Close to home: I've been
wearing glasses since age 13.
(That's a little self-portrait
in the middle.).

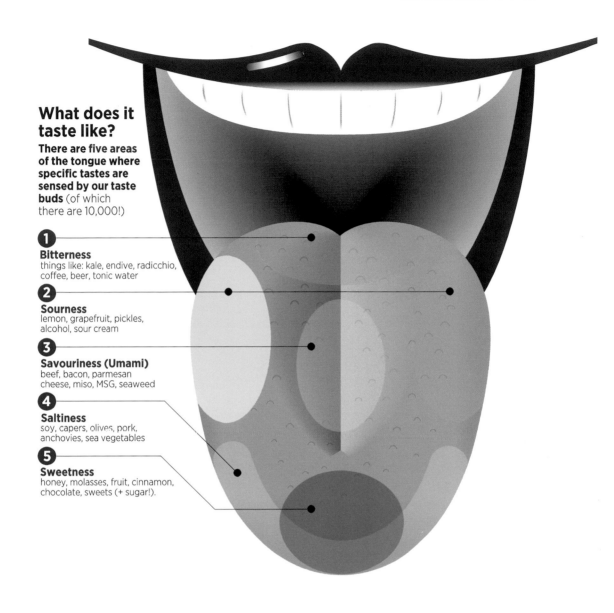

What does it taste like?

There are five areas of the tongue where specific tastes are sensed by our taste buds (of which there are 10,000!)

1

Bitterness
things like: kale, endive, radicchio, coffee, beer, tonic water

2

Sourness
lemon, grapefruit, pickles, alcohol, sour cream

3

Savouriness (Umami)
beef, bacon, parmesan cheese, miso, MSG, seaweed

4

Saltiness
soy, capers, olives, pork, anchovies, sea vegetables

5

Sweetness
honey, molasses, fruit, cinnamon, chocolate, sweets (+ sugar!).

A detail of a graphic adapted from Instant Expert, 2014. The book was how to be everything—from a bookbinder, a bouncer, a brewer, to a Casanova, and here, a food taster.

ISCHEMIC STROKE AND tPA: TIME IS OF THE ESSENCE

Ischemic stroke occurs when the blood supply to a part of the brain is blocked

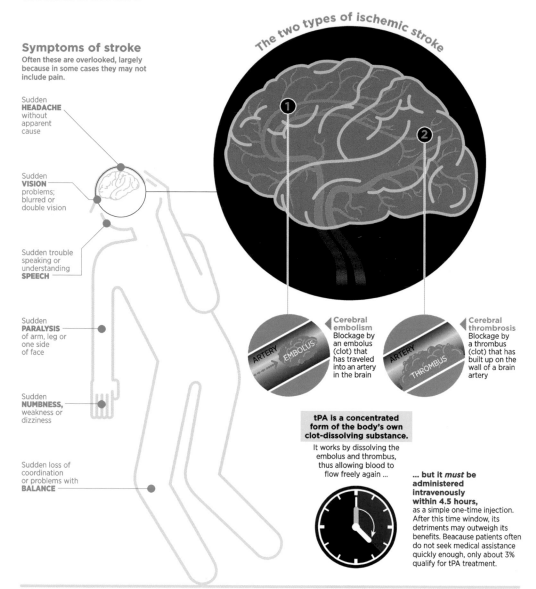

Symptoms of stroke
Often these are overlooked, largely because in some cases they may not include pain.

Sudden **HEADACHE** without apparent cause

Sudden **VISION** problems; blurred or double vision

Sudden trouble speaking or understanding **SPEECH**

Sudden **PARALYSIS** of arm, leg or one side of face

Sudden **NUMBNESS,** weakness or dizziness

Sudden loss of coordination or problems with **BALANCE**

The two types of ischemic stroke

① **Cerebral embolism**
Blockage by an embolus (clot) that has traveled into an artery in the brain

ARTERY EMBOLUS

② **Cerebral thrombrosis**
Blockage by a thrombus (clot) that has built up on the wall of a brain artery

ARTERY THROMBUS

tPA is a concentrated form of the body's own clot-dissolving substance.

It works by dissolving the embolus and thrombus, thus allowing blood to flow freely again ...

... but it *must* be administered intravenously within 4.5 hours, as a simple one-time injection. After this time window, its detriments may outweigh its benefits. Beacause patients often do not seek medical assistance quickly enough, only about 3% qualify for tPA treatment.

80% to 85% of all strokes are ischemic strokes

Above, for Northwestern (University) Magazine, 2011. (Art Director Christina Senese)

Right, an 8.5 x 11-inch factsheet about HPV (human papillomavirus) and cervical cancer for the American Social Health Association, that folded down to a small pocketable size. It was freely available in health clinics.

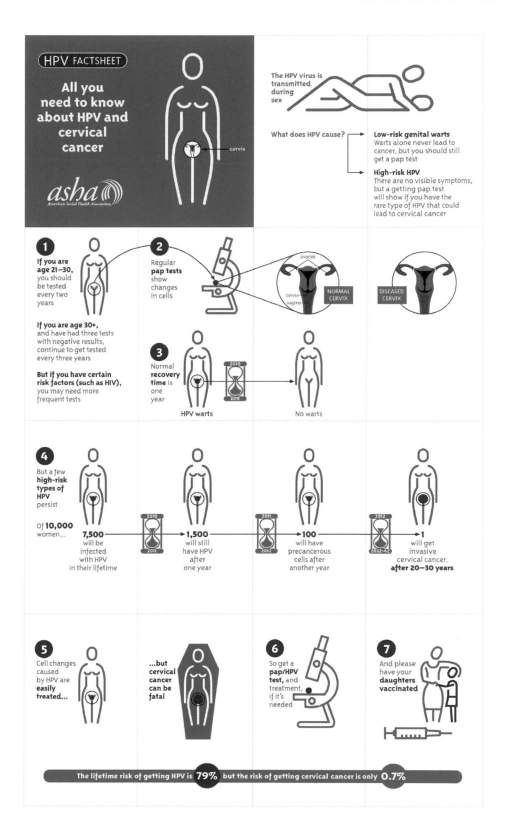

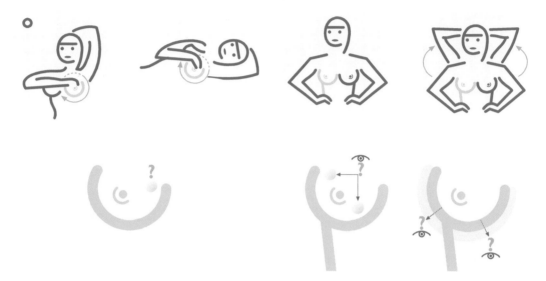

Adapted from Wordless Diagrams: how to do your own test for breast lumps.

In 2006, Eric Seidman, the Art Director of AARP Bulletin, and I proposed a feature, Wise Guy, that would run across the bottom of several consecutive pages. Composed of lists, small charts and facts, it added info to the main story above it on the pages. Shown here are two panels from the prototype. Another good idea that never got into print!

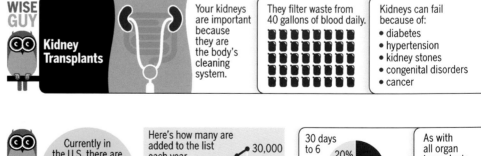

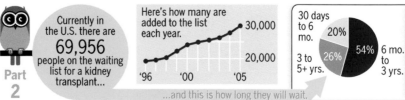

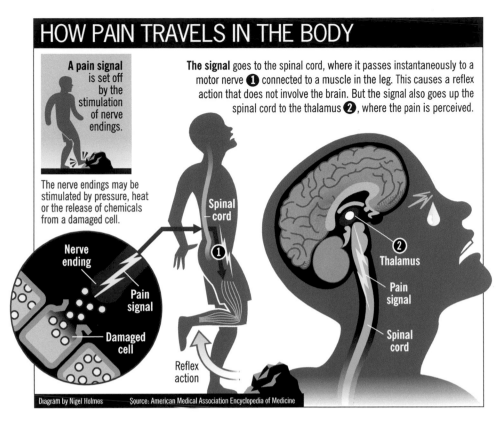

For a Time magazine special issue on medicine. (Art Director Marty Golon)

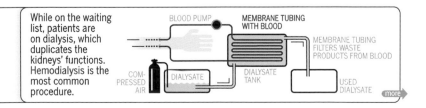

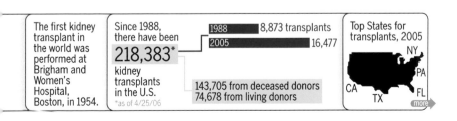

How to Cool Down Quickly

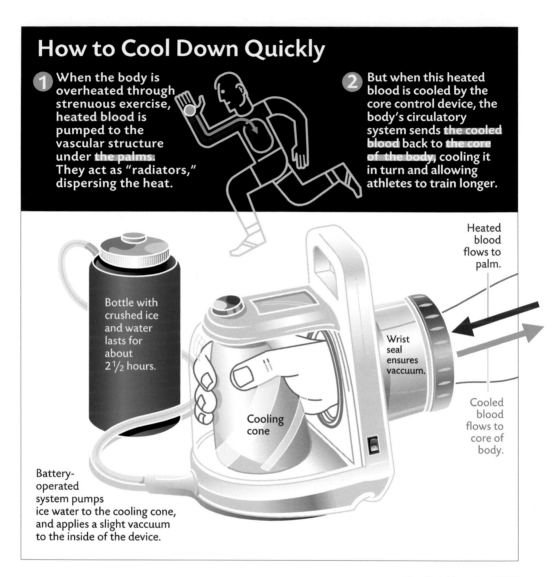

1 When the body is overheated through strenuous exercise, heated blood is pumped to the vascular structure under the palms. They act as "radiators," dispersing the heat.

2 But when this heated blood is cooled by the core control device, the body's circulatory system sends the cooled blood back to the core of the body, cooling it in turn and allowing athletes to train longer.

Heated blood flows to palm.

Bottle with crushed ice and water lasts for about 2½ hours.

Wrist seal ensures vaccuum.

Cooled blood flows to core of body.

Cooling cone

Battery-operated system pumps ice water to the cooling cone, and applies a slight vaccuum to the inside of the device.

Stanford Magazine, 2005.
(Art Director Bambi Nicklen).

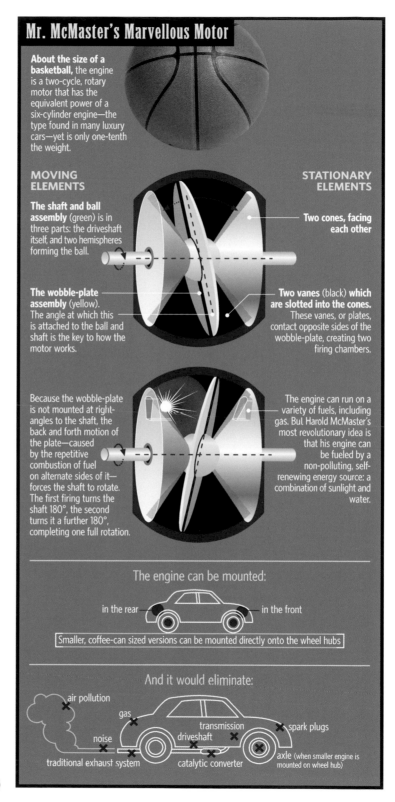

Mr. McMaster's Marvellous Motor

About the size of a basketball, the engine is a two-cycle, rotary motor that has the equivalent power of a six-cylinder engine—the type found in many luxury cars—yet is only one-tenth the weight.

MOVING ELEMENTS

The shaft and ball assembly (green) is in three parts: the driveshaft itself, and two hemispheres forming the ball.

The wobble-plate assembly (yellow). The angle at which this is attached to the ball and shaft is the key to how the motor works.

Because the wobble-plate is not mounted at right-angles to the shaft, the back and forth motion of the plate—caused by the repetitive combustion of fuel on alternate sides of it—forces the shaft to rotate. The first firing turns the shaft 180°, the second turns it a further 180°, completing one full rotation.

STATIONARY ELEMENTS

Two cones, facing each other

Two vanes (black) **which are slotted into the cones.** These vanes, or plates, contact opposite sides of the wobble-plate, creating two firing chambers.

The engine can run on a variety of fuels, including gas. But Harold McMaster's most revolutionary idea is that his engine can be fueled by a non-polluting, self-renewing energy source: a combination of sunlight and water.

The engine can be mounted:

in the rear — in the front

Smaller, coffee-can sized versions can be mounted directly onto the wheel hubs

And it would eliminate:

air pollution
gas
noise
traditional exhaust system
transmission
driveshaft
catalytic converter
spark plugs
axle (when smaller engine is mounted on wheel hub)

*From Business 2.0
(Art Director Susan Casey)*

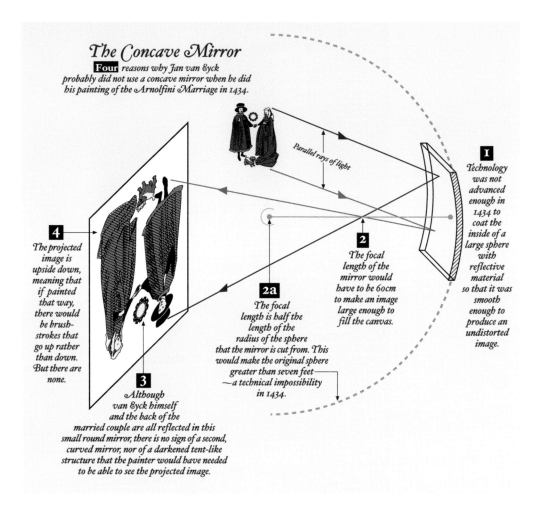

The Concave Mirror

Four reasons why Jan van Eyck probably did not use a concave mirror when he did his painting of the Arnolfini Marriage in 1434.

Parallel rays of light

1 Technology was not advanced enough in 1434 to coat the inside of a large sphere with reflective material so that it was smooth enough to produce an undistorted image.

2 The focal length of the mirror would have to be 60cm to make an image large enough to fill the canvas.

2a The focal length is half the length of the radius of the sphere that the mirror is cut from. This would make the original sphere greater than seven feet —a technical impossibility in 1434.

3 Although van Eyck himself and the back of the married couple are all reflected in this small round mirror, there is no sign of a second, curved mirror, nor of a darkened tent-like structure that the painter would have needed to be able to see the projected image.

4 The projected image is upside down, meaning that if painted that way, there would be brushstrokes that go up rather than down. But there are none.

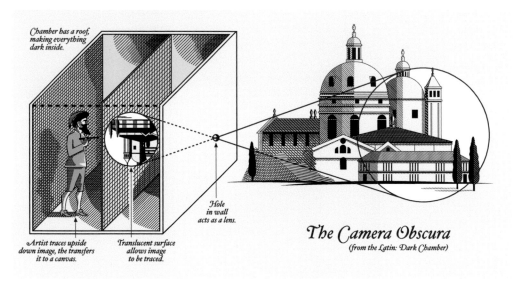

Chamber has a roof, making everything dark inside.

Artist traces upside down image, the transfers it to a canvas.

Translucent surface allows image to be traced.

Hole in wall acts as a lens.

The Camera Obscura
(from the Latin: Dark Chamber)

Recycling

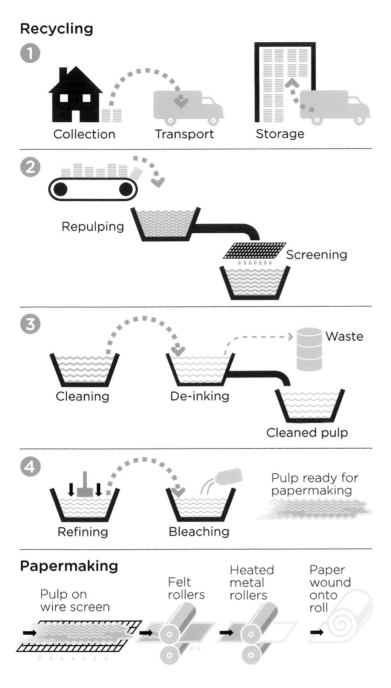

① Collection   Transport   Storage

② Repulping   Screening

③ Cleaning   De-inking   Waste   Cleaned pulp

④ Refining   Bleaching   Pulp ready for papermaking

Papermaking

Pulp on wire screen   Felt rollers   Heated metal rollers   Paper wound onto roll

For National Geographic's Green Guide, published in 2008, this diagram shows the process of recycling paper from collection to being made back into paper. (Art Director, Marty Ittner.)

Left, for an article in Stanford Magazine about David Hockney's theories of how old master paintings may have been created with mechanical devices that helped artists make accurate renderings, I used old-fashioned cross-hatching (and font) to give the diagrams a look that somewhat matched the period. (Art Director Bambi Nicklen)

A final piece from Attaché magazine, 2000. As with other Attaché graphics, the Greek chorus chimed in—this time I'm let off the hook for simplifying the information. The magazine was intended for casual readers, not a manual for their car!

SEE WHAT YOUR PISTONS ARE UP TO

1 **Intake stroke:** with the inlet valve open, the descending piston draws a mixture of gas and air into the cylinder.

2 **Compression stroke:** both valves close; the rising piston compresses the mixture.

3 **Power stroke:** a spark ignites the mixture; the explosion forces the piston down.

4 **Exhaust stroke:** the rising piston discharges spent gases through the open exhaust valve, then the cycle starts again. The same four-stroke process happens in each cylinder.

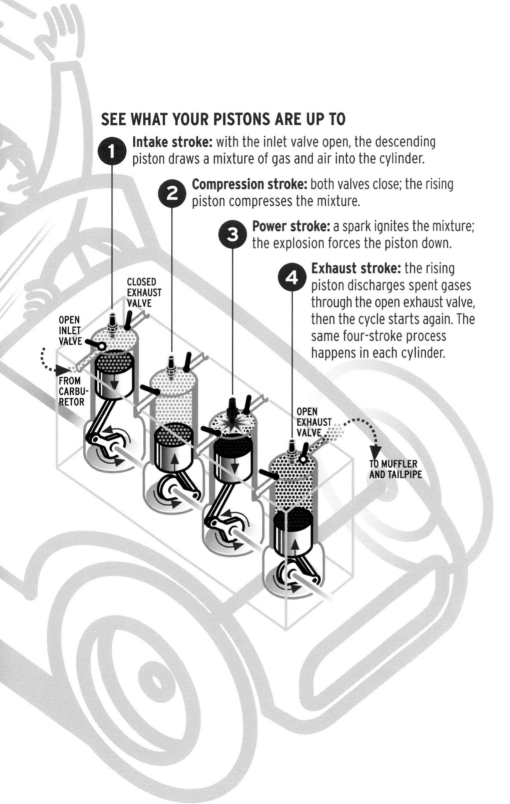

CLOSED
EXHAUST
VALVE

OPEN
INLET
VALVE

FROM
CARBU-
RETOR

OPEN
EXHAUST
VALVE

TO MUFFLER
AND TAILPIPE

OK, that's enough.

Chartoons

To the Editor, TIME Magazine. Dear Sir, with your 7 and 14 April [1980] issues, Holmes' charts have gone from being merely puzzling and ignorable to indecipherable and downright annoying. I have long since decided to ignore Holmes' cute charts, but your permitting him to indulge his fancy in the pages of TIME is resulting in less information for my money … I would appreciate it if you would allay one suspicion—is Holmes the publisher's son-in-law?

To the Editor, TIME Magazine. Dear Sir, it has become increasingly obvious that Nigel Holmes has aspirations toward the field of cartooning. I hope the January 19 [1981] issue satisfies his urge and he can get back to charts and graphs and leave the horsies and witches and all the other funny little creatures to the boys at Disney Studios.

Four million people read *Time* magazine when I worked there. There were bound to be some of them who hated my work! (I did get nice letters, too.)

A chart about the price of diamonds was the best answer to why it would be hopeless for me to have 'aspirations toward the field of cartooning.' Everyone who saw it thought it was Marilyn Monroe, who sang *Diamonds are a Girl's Best Friend* in the movie *Gentlemen Prefer Blondes*. But I had drawn Carol Channing, the star of the Broadway play of the same name, in 1949. Here are my sketches and the final piece. I guess it didn't look like either actress!

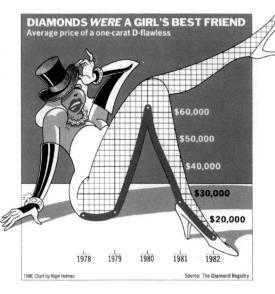

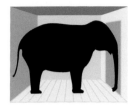

Is that an elephant in the room? If you are a seasoned infographic or data visualization designer, you are probably familiar with the writings of Edward Tufte, and you may have read that he referred to the *Diamonds* chart as *chartjunk* in his 1990 book *Envisioning Information*. He's entitled to his opinion, of course. And among the roughly 1,000 charts that I did at *Time*, some of them *were* over-illustrated.

But I believe that none of my charts or graphics trivialized the data, which was scrupulously checked by wonderful fact-checking researchers, principally Noel McCoy and Deborah Wells. Tufte simply misunderstood my audience.

He was writing from an academic standpoint, and he urged his readers that his 'rules' were universal and should *always* be used—when making graphics for *any* audience. I was making charts for the non-specialist readers of a general-interest magazine, and I knew that *Time*'s readers might not be completely versed in all aspects of business, or medicine, or science, and that they appreciated a little visual help in understanding those concepts. That was not *chartjunk*, it was *charthelp*, as was demonstrated by academic papers published years later. Of course, if the illustrated parts of a chart distract from an understanding of the data, then the chart fails. However, if the illustrated parts of a chart help a reader to (1) instantly see what the chart is about, and (2) offer pointers as to its meaning, then those additions are not junk.

I contacted Tufte in 1990 after the publication of *Envisioning Information,* but did not get a reply. Now, some 30 years later, in an effort to give him an opportunity to comment on what I have said here, I sent him the text you are reading here as a courtesy. Again, he did not reply. Elephant leaves the room.

The American philosopher John Dewey said this about scientists, but I think it applies to infographic rule-makers: *'We are not called upon to defend them, for their work is in the past; we are not called upon to attack them, for our work is in the future.'* (Much of my work is in the past, so that would apply to me, too, if I had issued a set of rules about chartmaking.)

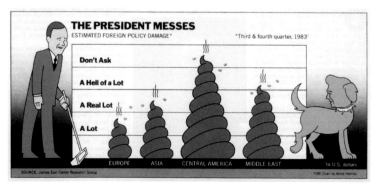

The best compliment I ever got was to be included in National Lampoon's parody of Time. The fake charts had this lovely credit: Mobil Holmes. They were drawn by Philip A. Scheuer, a contributing artist at the Lampoon.

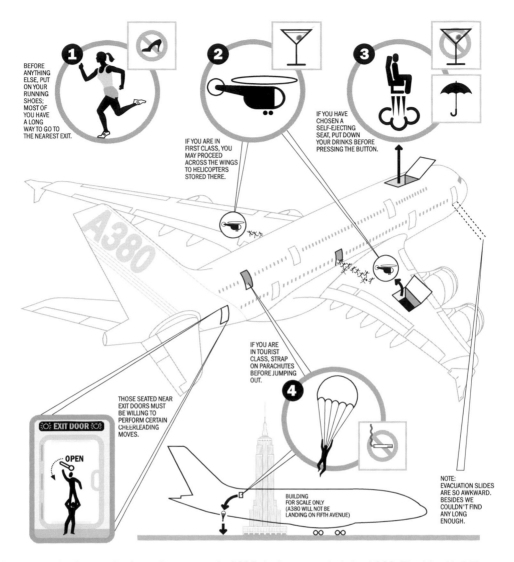

I've been asked to make faux charts, too. In 2005, Airbus unveiled the A380. *The New York Times* invited me to imagine the emergency instructions for such a large plane *(above)*.

Also in *The New York Times*, for Father's Day in 1999, the *Style Section* Art Director Richard Aloisio sent me a story about a daughter and son thinking about what to give their dad that wasn't the typical Father's Day gift—another boring tie.

Dad was an inventor of sorts. All I had to do was to diagram his kids' description of a self-operated cat toilet that their Dad had invented. I included a tie, anyway, just for cliché's sake.

From 2013 to 2020, Robert Priest and Grace Lee wrote and designed *Eight by Eight*, a magazine about football (soccer), and they allowed me to have some diagrammatic fun within its beautifully crafted pages. For a piece about proposed ways to improve referees' calls about handling dubious goals, I added this silly bit at the end of my otherwise factual graphic.

KITTYBALLS

A kitten is placed inside the ball ❶ (with adequate, but aerodynamically insignificant, breathing holes) ❷. The goal-line is impregnated with an intense, concentrated fish odor ❸, so that when the ball crosses it, the kitten mews loudly in anticipation of a tasty meal ❹. Small microphones inside the ball relay the sound to the ref, players and fans. The developers of the KittyBalls system are working on autotuning the somewhat plaintive meowing so that what is actually broadcast is a full-throated "GOOOOOOAL."

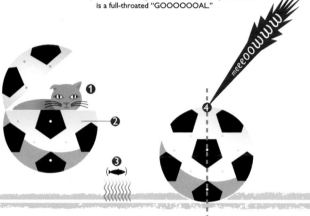

Something I didn't mention about live performances was that at the end of a lecture I often sang a song, usually with my words about graphics that had something to do with the talk, set to a well-known tune. One day in the bathroom, I had noticed that my *Dry Idea* deodorant had a price sticker pasted onto the container exactly on top of the letter Y in *Dry*. Dr. Idea was born, and sung, rather poorly, on the stage at Stanford University. But there was a point: the good doctor will help you find ideas in surprising places. Keep an open mind. (By the way, if you open yourself up to such humiliation—singing when you aren't that good—the audience mostly loves it. Then they tell you to stick to your day job.)

The pie chart comes in for some hefty ribbing in the infographic world, particularly on Twitter. Whatever you think of the pie as a charting method—me: it's good, as long as there are no more than six or seven parts, and they add up to a hundred—pies are all around us. (And should always be round.) These are my own iterations of images that make fun of pies. I don't know who to acknowledge, but thank you for the smiles.

And we know it's good for you to smile, because science says so. *(See previous chapter.)*

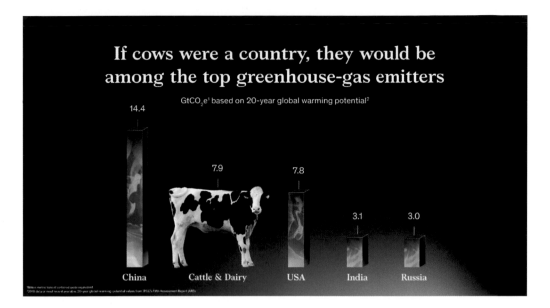

Sometimes an infographic can look like a joke but contains real, serious data. Look at this bar chart, *(above),* about greenhouse-gas emitters. It was designed by Jason Forrest, Gabrielle Merite and Gergo Varga for McKinsey & Company. OK, it breaks the 'rules' of chart-making: three-dimensional bars with tops that fuzz exact data points; unequal bar widths (and how!) …who cares—the point is very clear. I love it.

In my brief history of pictorial infographics in Chapter 2, I'm critical of abstract data visualizations that are worthy data representations but are overly complex. In print, I feel some visualizations lack the editing needed to help readers and users understand why the information is relevant to them and their own lives. In conference presentations I had fun with the difference between data visualization, represented by The Data-Rich Porcupine *(manylinus bewilderus)*, and infographics, represented by The Edited Zebra *(infograficus understanda).* The idea was to acknowledge the difference, while joking about it. Perhaps both camps—the shaggy porcupines and the organized zebras—take ourselves a bit too seriously.

THE DATA-RICH PORCUPINE
(manylinus bewilderus)

THE EDITED ZEBRA
(infograficus understanda)

Don't do this!

It's confession time. I have made some awful graphics. So rather than point the finger at anyone else's less-than-excellent charts, I'll point it at myself. Why? Because everyone has blind spots, and sometimes, in an effort to make a point, I've crossed a line. Doubtless eager, critical formalists will pounce on these examples and say: 'See, he *does make chartjunk*.' To which I reply, you are right (some of the time). These charts from *Time* are a don't-do-this warning.

Please don't overdo the illustration.
I was trained as an illustrator, but this 'illustration' got in the way of the data 'Nuff said.

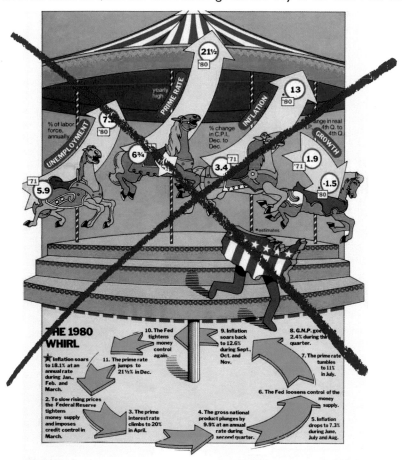

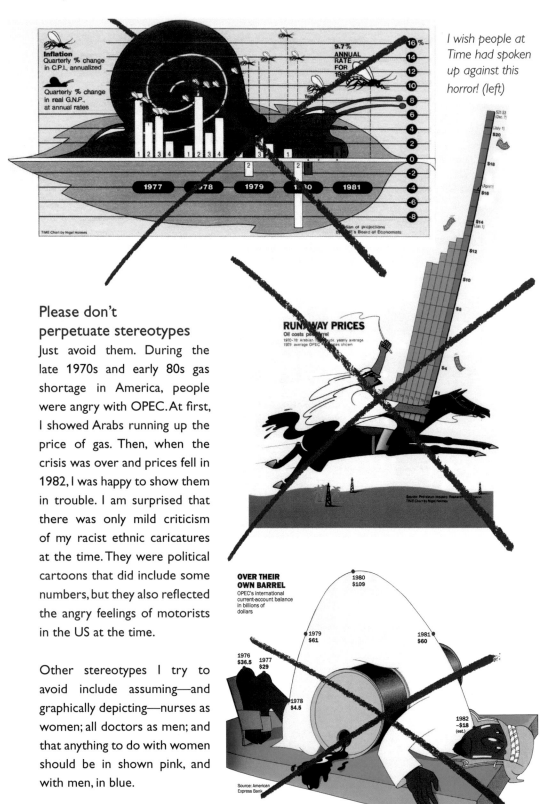

I wish people at Time had spoken up against this horror! (left)

Please don't perpetuate stereotypes

Just avoid them. During the late 1970s and early 80s gas shortage in America, people were angry with OPEC. At first, I showed Arabs running up the price of gas. Then, when the crisis was over and prices fell in 1982, I was happy to show them in trouble. I am surprised that there was only mild criticism of my racist ethnic caricatures at the time. They were political cartoons that did include some numbers, but they also reflected the angry feelings of motorists in the US at the time.

Other stereotypes I try to avoid include assuming—and graphically depicting—nurses as women; all doctors as men; and that anything to do with women should be in shown pink, and with men, in blue.

Please don't try to make a picture out of everything.

I've already suggested that clichés to show the ups and downs of the stock market as mountain ranges and rollercoasters should be ditched. Here's my worst idea (from the mid-70s):   America as a fetus. Thankfully, enough people at *Time* loudly objected as my rough sketch made the editorial rounds; the finished piece did not run in the magazine.

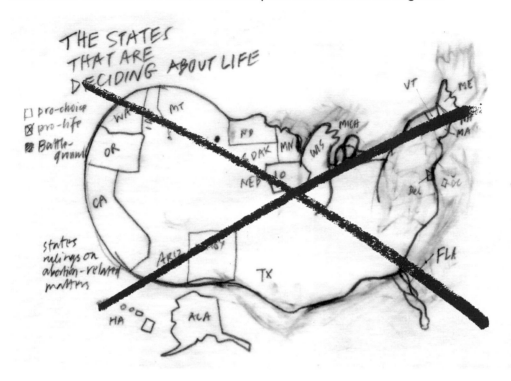

The problem is this: an infographic causing moral outrage, one that steps on religious opinions, or puts forward a political and moral viewpoint, such as the abortion map, should be stopped. I hold strong views, but this was beyond the pale. However, if a graphic merely offends people's aesthetic sense, like the slug, it's just an ugly thing, and people turn the page. You, the artist, have to be the judge of when to restrain yourself.

Since I can never resist a tidbit of explanation when there's an interesting one, the metaphor 'beyond the pale'—meaning something that's outside society's boundaries of acceptable behavior—is derived from the Latin word for a pointed wooden post lined up with others to form a fence that you should not cross. Don't go beyond the pale.

Please don't think that dressing up charts, especially pies, with 3-d effects will make your graphics more joyful.

Whenever a client, or editor, suggests that making a chart three-dimensional will help it to 'jump off the page,' please say no. I like pies, but I want them to stay on the page so I can read them accurately.

Please don't forget to have fun.
This is perhaps the most important don't. If you enjoy what you are doing, it will shine through in your work, and connect you to your audience.

I'm not sure where I read this, but it's a lovely motto:
Be reasonable.
Be kind.
Be funny.

Thank you for reading.
Now get going and make joyful infographics!

Appendix

(It's usually on the right.)

Contrary to popular thought, the appendix is not where your body shunts all the bad stuff it doesn't need (cherry pips, swallowed gum). But why it's there at all is a bit of a mystery. One theory: evolution has rendered it useless. The appendix gets preemptively removed in case you get a pain in your tummy, and certainly *when* you get a pain in your tummy. I'm grateful that the word surgeons (aka editors) haven't removed this one, which has some stuff in it that might seem to have little to do with this book, but which is fun nevertheless.

Random images

I used a lot of adhesive-backed sheets of Letratone and Zipatone in my artwork before the Mac gave me all the dots, squiggles, and tints I could dream of. I tried to match the half-tone dot screen of whatever publication I was appearing in so that the grays in my graphics looked the same as the gray tones in photographs. But sometimes, for a different effect, I deliberately used a larger dot screen. And there were other patterns available; I liked the wavy lines. When I was asked to do a simple black and white line drawing for a coloring book I used a whole sheet of Letratone's undulating lines to stand in for very neatly plowed furrows. I wonder if anyone colored in anything other than the tractor?

Doing something other than your infographics day job can be both relaxing and invigorating. There are a couple of non-deadline things I do that may or may not influence my graphic work. One is making (almost daily) collages. These often start with a scrap of color or a shape I see in the daily newspaper, and are generally finished within a few minutes. It's a bit like the surrealists' idea of automatic art: you gather a few scraps of paper; arrange them into some sort of shape, usually abstract, without much thought; see what's there, and glue the pieces down. That's it. There's no purpose to this activity, and few people see the results.

A good substitute for the wavy lines of yore, (or at least of the previous page, made 50 years ago) is the pattern printed on the inside of some business envelopes. It softens the blow of a big bill if you can use the envelope it came in.

I like the contrast between roughly torn edges and sharp, cut ones. This sort of exercise gives you a chance to widen your palette, with colors you might not put together in information graphics, and also to appreciate the importance of pure black.

When I was at art school, I loved the physicality of lino- and wood-cutting. Today, it's just a hobby, but still related to image-making. I made a two-color lino cut of Sheemia, a neighbor's cat who came to visit me most days and posed nicely for photos while walking all over my computer keyboard. Then, just as abruptly as she had appeared outside the door to the office, she would go and sit by it, asking to leave. Sheemia's owner had young children whose name for her was Meatball; to me she was the sweetest and most welcome visitor, and not a meatball at all.

Here she is again in a how-to-draw-an-icon-of-a-cat demo:

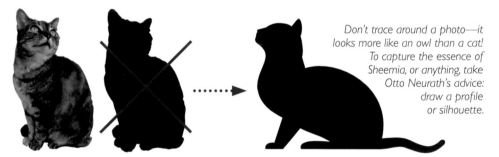

Don't trace around a photo—it looks more like an owl than a cat! To capture the essence of Sheemia, or anything, take Otto Neurath's advice: draw a profile or silhouette.

Wooden toys

These are basically exercises in simplifying. The wood itself constrains what you are able to do with it—unless you are an expert woodworker/carver—but you can use what might seem like a limitation to make friendly toys for your kids (or grandkids).

An admiring nod to information designer Ladislav Sutnar and artist Joaquín Torres-García. Both made beautiful wooden children's toys.

An optical trick

Like the white arrow hidden between the e and the x in the Fedex logo, the white 8 inside the eight of diamonds is a nice surprise when you first see it. (Afterwards, you can never unsee it.) It works because the concavy diamond shapes on playing cards aren't what a designer would produce when asked to draw a diamond.

A card trick

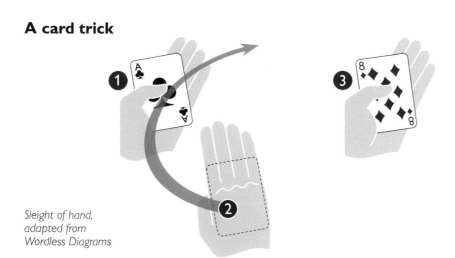

Sleight of hand, adapted from Wordless Diagrams

Lists

You've seen lists—not the boring ones, fun ones, many posted by Neil Kaye on Twitter. For instance, a list of palindromes (*Do geese see god?*); a list of the longest words with no repeated letters (*uncopyrightable*); words with vowels in alphabetical order (*abstemious*); words with the most of each letter (for i: *indivisibility*); portmanteau words (*racinos* for horse-racing casinos; *quixonic* for odd-sounding music).

My favorite list is the Shakespeare Insult Kit, *(right)*.

Take one unflattering jibe from each column and preface the result with 'Thou.' Endless fun.

More smiles

I took this picture in the Metropolitan Museum of Art, in New York. It's a sculpture from the 6th century BC.

1	2	3
artless	bat-fowling	apple-john
bawdy	beef-witted	baggeage
beslubbering	beetle-headed	barnacle
bootless	boil-brained	bladder
churlish	clapper-clawed	bugbear
cockered	clay-brained	bum-bailey
clouted	common-kissing	canker-blossom
currish	crook-pated	clack-dish
dankish	dread-bolted	clotpole
droning	earth-vexing	coxcomb
errant	elf-skinned	codpiece
fobbing	fen-sucked	dewberry
frothy	flap-mouthed	flap-dragon
gleeking	fly-bitten	flax-wench
goatish	fool-born	flirt-gill
gorbellied	guts-griping	foot-licker
impertinent	half-faced	fustilarian
infectious	hasty-witted	giglet
jarring	hedge-born	gudgeon
loggerheaded	hell-hated	hedge-pig
lumpish	idle-headed	horn-beast
mammering	ill-breeding	hugger-mugger
mangled	knotty-pated	lewdster
mewling	milk-livered	lout
paunchy	motley-minded	maggot-pie
pribbling	onion-eyed	malt-worm
puking	plume-plucked	mammet
puny	pottle-deep	measle
qualling	pox-marked	minnow
rank	reeling-ripe	miscreant
reeky	rough-hewn	moldwarp
ruttish	rude-growing	mumble-news
saucy	rump-fed	nut-hook
spleeny	shard-borne	pignut
spongy	sheep-biting	puttock
surly	spur-galed	pumpion
tottering	swag-bellied	ratsbane
vain	tardy-gaited	scut
villainous	tickle-brained	skainsmate
warped	toad-spotted	strumpet
weedy	urchin-snouted	varlot
yeasty	weather-bitten	whey-face

I had always understood that painted portraits of people never showed them smiling—it was too hard for the sitter to hold a smile for a long time. So what was going on with a smiling statue?

The smile used by Greek sculptors is called the *archaic smile*, and it suggests that the person depicted was alive and 'infused with a sense of well-being,' according to that most excellent source, Wikipedia.

There's a whole room of Cypriot smiling statues like this one at the Met. As I've said elsewhere in this book, smiles are contagious. Test it for yourself.

Accidental finds

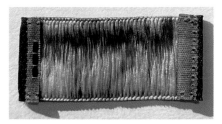

I'm amused by the cyclists who whiz down the road outside our house, wearing ads all over their shiny, spandexed bodies. I imagine they are fantasizing about riding in the *Tour de France,* although the expressions on their faces don't give the impression that it's a particularly enjoyable fantasy. I hope they are being paid to look like speeding billboards.

Personally, I don't care to advertise what I'm wearing or carrying, so I avoid labels on t-shirts, tote bags and anything else. But sometimes I get a little thrill when removing labels, *(below),* and it reminds me to keep eyes open for accidental treasures.

I have nothing against LLBean; I just don't want to be a walking ad for them.

This is what's on the back of that label: blow it up and hang it in a gallery!

Inconsistency

I've lived and worked on both sides of the Atlantic, and I'm caught in the middle, initially mixed up about how to spell some words (*humor, humour*), or not knowing the American meaning of others. (I was upset when an art director told me a piece of mine was *quite* nice, because in England *quite* would mean *do it again.*) Or clinging to old pronunciation (*tomarto*), and not knowing what to call some punctuation (*full stop* for *period*; *inverted commas* for *quotes*), and so on.

Then I remember the wonderful Ralph Waldo Emerson quote '*A foolish consistency is the hobgoblin of little minds…*' I do not mean to say that text editors have little minds—it's their job to bring a certain consistency to text—but I am increasingly influenced by the opinions of the American linguist John McWhorter, who regards language as ever-evolving. He says we shouldn't look down on colloquialisms or regard different ways of saying things as 'wrong,' and he's even making room for 'like' (currently used in every spoken sentence, it seems) when it has nothing to do with actually *liking* anything. Mr. McWhorter urges us to think hard about the use of words, and how they change over time.

I hope you are not offended by my grammatical (or graphical) inconsistency, but if you are, I'll take responsibility, requote Emerson and blame it on McWhorter!

Books, articles, links

Introduction
Thoughts on Design, Paul Rand, Wittenborn Schultz, New York, 1947
Ornament and Crime, Adolf Loos [lecture], https://en.wikipedia.org/wiki/Ornament_and_Crime
Eyes on The News, Mario Garcia and Pegie Stark, Poynter Institute, St Petersburg, 1991
Nigel Holmes on Information Design, Steven Heller, Jorge Pinto Books, 2006

Influences
Holmes of the Humber, Tony Watts, Lodestar Books, London, 2009
The Complete Nonsense of Edward Lear, Faber and Faber, London, 1947
The Parrots, Edward Lear, The Complete Plates, Taschen, Cologne, 2018
Comic Drawing, W.W. (Bill) Sillince, Sir Isaac Pitman, London, 1950
Running Commentary, Fougasse, Methuen, London, 1941
Eadweard Muybridge, The Stanford Years, Exhibition Catalog, Stanford U., 1972
River of Shadows, Rebecca Solnit, Viking Penguin, New York, 2003
Eric Gill, Man of Flesh and Spirit, Malcolm Yorke, Universe Books, New York, 1982
Eric Gill, Fiona MacCarthy, Faber and Faber, London, 1989
The Goon Show, https://en.wikipedia.org/wiki/The_Goon_Show
Monty Python's Flying Circus, https://en.wikipedia.org/wiki/Monty_Python%27s_Flying_Circus
Civilisation, Kenneth Clark [TV series and related book] BBC, London, 1969-70
Rediscovering the Blazingly Bright Colors of Ancient Sculptures, Anika Burgess, Atlas Obscura, 2018
Gods in Color: Polychromy in the Ancient World, Vinzenz Brinkman & Others, Prestel Publishing, 2017

Pictorial data through the ages
Primitive Art, L. Adam, Pelican Books, London, 1942
From Cave Painting to Comic Strip, Lancelot Hogben, Chanticleer Press, New York, 1949
The Meaning of Art, Herbert Read, Faber & Faber, London, 1951
The Story of Art, E.H. Gombrich, Phaidon, London, 1960
Icon and Idea, Herbert Read, Schocken Books, New York, 1965
The Ascent of Man, Jacob Bronowski, Little Brown, Boston, 1973
The Creative Explosion, John E. Pfeiffer, Harper & Row, 1982
Altamira, The Origin of Art, Miguel Garcia Guinea, Madrid, 1977
The Mind in the Cave, David Lewis-Williams, Thames & Hudson, London, 2002
The Cave Painters, Gregory Curtis, Knopf, New York, 2006
Visual Language, Nigel Holmes, privately published, 2011
Sapiens, Yuval Noah Harari, Harper Perennial, New York, 2015
This is the Voice, John Colapinto, Simon & Schuster, New York, 2021
Behold the Stone Age, Robert Hughes, Time, 2/13/1995

Homo Artisticus, Arthur Danto, The Nation, 2/20/1995

New Lascaux a Forgery? Alexander Cockburn, The Nation, 2/20/1995

Allegory of the Cave, letters from Danto and Cockburn, The Nation, 4/24/1995

Stone Age Menageries, Virginia Morell, Audubon, May/June, 1995

First Impressions, Judith Thurman, The New Yorker, 6/23/2008

Images of the Ice Age, Alexander Marshack, Archeology, July/August, 1995

Cross-Modality Information Transfer: A Hypothesis about the Relationship among Prehistoric Cave Paintings, Symbolic Thinking, and the Emergence of Language, Shigeru Miyagawa, Cora Lesure, Vitor A Nóbrega, Frontiers in Psychology, 2/20/2018

Neanderthals, the World's First Misunderstood Artists, Carl Zimmer, NY Times, 2/22/2018

Researchers Snuffle Up Rare Work of Cave Art, Becky Ferreira, NY Times, 1/19/2021

Before They Spoke, They Had to Listen, Sabrina Imbler, New York Times, 3/9/2021

Commercial and Political Atlas, William Playfair, 1786, London [Third edition (1801) available as a facsimile, with an introduction by Howard Wainer and Ian Spence, Cambridge University Press, New York, 2005]

Look at the World, The Fortune Atlas for World Strategy, Richard Edes Harrison, Fortune, 1944

Mr Beck's Underground Map, Ken Garland, Capita; Transport, London, 1994

Cartography, Kenneth Field, Esri Press, Redlands, CA, 2018

Thematic Mapping, Kenneth Field, Esri Press, Redlands, CA, 2022

International Picture Language, Otto Neurath, Kegan Paul, Trench, Trubner, London, 1936

Modern Man in the Making, Otto Neurath, Knopf, New York and London, 1939

Otto Neurath, Empiricism and Sociology, Marie Neurath and Robert Cohen, D. Reidel Publishing Company, Dordrecht, Holland, 1973

Graphic Communication Through Isotype, University of Reading, J.A. Edwards and Michael Twyman,) 1975

Symbols for Education and Statistics, Gerd Arntz and Kees Broos, Mart, Spruijt Uitgever, 1979

Design Writing Research, Ellen Lupton and J Abbot Miller, Princeton Architectural Press, New York, 1996

Otto Neurath's Universal Silhouettes, George Pendle, Shadows, Issue 24, 2006/7

Otto Neurath, The Language of the Global Polis, Nader Vossoughian, NAi, 2008

Lovely Language, Ed Annink and Max Bruinsma, Veenman, Rotterdam, 2008

The Transformer, Marie Neurath and Robin Kinross, Hyphen Press, London, 2009

Gerd Arntz, Graphic Designer, Ed Annink and Max Bruinsma, 010 Publishers, Rotterdam, 2010

Isotype, Design and Contexts, Christopher Burke, Eric Kindel, Sue Walker, Hyphen Press, London, 2013

From Hieroglyphics to Isotype, Otto Neurath, Hyphen Press, London, 2010

Image Factories: Kahn, Neurath, Various Editors, Spector Books, Leipzig, 2018

Reading Isotype, Ellen Lupton, Design Discourse, Chicago, 1989

Otto Neurath's Rhetoric of Neutrality, Jae Young Lee, Visible Language, 2008

Principles and Practices of Neurath's Picture Language, Ahti-Veikko Pietarinen, Visible Language 42.2, 2010

Isotype, Recent Publications, Robin Kinross, Hyphen Press, 2018

Gerd Arntz, lecture by Kees Broos, Moscow, 2018, Text published in Designabilities, dutchhistory.nl, 2019

Design Writing Research, Ellen Lupton and J. Abbott Miller, Princeton Architectural Press, New York, 1996

Losing Propositions, Adam Kirsch, The New Yorker, 10/19/2020

Fritz Kahn, Uta and Thilo von Debschitz, Taschen, Cologne, 2013

1066 And All That, W.C. Sellar and R.J. Yeatman, Methuen, London, 1930

Dear Data, Stephanie Posavec and Giorgia Lupi, Princeton Architectural Press, 2016

I am a book. I am a portal to the universe, Stefanie Posavec and Miriam Quick, Particular Books, 2020

Nine Ways

Cruel Pies: The Inhumanity of Technical Illustrations, Sam Dragga and Dan Voss,
  Technical Communication, 8/2001

Connecting with the Dots, Jacob Harris, 1/15/2015, https://source.opennews.org/articles/connecting-dots/

Do No Harm Guide: Applying Equity Awareness in Data Visualization, Alice Feng & and Jonathan Schwabish,
  Urban Institute, 6/9/2021 https://www.urban.org/research/publication/do-no-harm-guide-applying-
  equity-awareness-data-visualization/

Six Ways to Bring Empathy into your Data, Alice Feng and Jonathan Schwabish, Nightingale, 6/10/2021
  https://nightingaledvs.com/author/alice-feng/

PolicyViz podcast episode 208 conversation between host John Schwabish and Frank Elavsky,
  12/28/2021 https://policyviz.com/podcast/episode-208-frank-elavsky/https://github.com/dataviza11y/
  resources#readme/

How to Lie with Statistics, Darrell Huff, WW Norton, New York, 1954

Connections, James Burke, Little Brown, London, 1978

The Cartoon Guide to Statistics, Larry Gonick and Woolcott Smith, HarperPerennial, New York, 1993

The Funny Little Man, Virginia Smith, Van Nostrand Reinhold, New York, 1993

Visual Function, Paul Mijksenaar, 010 Publishers, Rotterdam, 1997

Wordless Diagrams, Nigel Holmes, Bloomsbury USA, 2005

The Laws of Simplicity, John Maeda, MIT Press, Cambridge, 2006

The Functional Art, Alberto Cairo, New Riders, 2013

The Truthful Art, Alberto Cairo, New Riders, 2016

Our Font is Made of People, Alberto Cairo & Scott Klein, opennews.org, 2/2/2018

How Charts Lie, Alberto Cairo, WW Norton, New York, 2019

Mortality, Richard Saul Wurman and Nigel Holmes, 2019

Info We Trust, R. J. Andrew, Wiley, Hoboken, 2019

How to Make the World Add Up, Tim Harford, Bridge Street Press, 2020

Visualizing with Text, Richard Brath, CRC Press, 2021

Better Data Visualizations, Jonathan Schwabish, Columbia U. Press. New York, 2021

In Germany, Karl Marx and Elvis Direct Traffic, Laura Kiniry, Atlas Obscura, 8/24/2021

The Science of Visual Data Communication: What Works, Steven L. Franconeri et al., Psychological Science
  in the Public Interest, 12/15/2021 https://journals.sagepub.com/stoken/default

Information Design Workbook, Kim Baer, Rockport, MA, revised and updated, 2021

The Timetables of History, Bernard Grun, Simon & Schuster, New York, 1991

Icons

Semantography (Blissymbolics), C.K. Bliss, Sydney, 1966

Shepherd's glossary of graphic signs and symbols, Walter Shepherd, Dover, New York, 1971

Symbol Sourcebook, Henry Dreyfuss, McGraw-Hill, 1972

A Treasury of German Trademarks (Volumes One and Two), Leslie Cabarga,
  Art Direction Book Company, New York, 1982 & 1985

Designing Pictorial Symbols, Nigel Holmes with Rose DeNeve, Watson-Guptill, New York, 1985

Pictogram Design, Yukio Ota, Kashiwashobo, Tokyo, 1987

Kanji Pictographix, Michael Rowley, Stone Bridge Press, Berkeley, 1992

Genesis, Juli Gudehus, Lars Müller Publishers, 1992

Niko! The Smiley Collection, Tota Enomoto, Shoeisha, Tokyo, 1993

Drawing to Explain, Nigel Holmes, 1998

Iconic Communication, Masoud Yazdani and Philip Barker (editors), Intellect Books, 2000

Information Design Journal, Vol. 10, no. 2, pp 133–143, Nigel Holmes, 2001

Wayfinding at Schiphol, Paul Mijksenaar, Amsterdam, 2008

In the Land of Invented Languages, Arika Okrent, Spiegel & Grau, New York, 2009

Who Made That? (Olympic Rings), Pagan Kennedy, New York Times Magazine, 7/15/2012

Who Made That? (Emoticon), Pagan Kennedy, New York Times Magazine, 11/25/2012

How the Valentine's Day Heart Got its Shape, Olivia B. Waxman, Time.com, 2/13/2017

The Original Seed Pod That May Have Inspired the Heart Shape, Cara Giamo, Atlas Obscura, 2/13/2017

In Heraldry, Hearts Can Symbolize Everything from Lily Pads to Testicles, Eric Grundhauser,
    Atlas Obscura, 2/16/2017

Book from the Ground, Xu Bing, MIT Press, Cambridge, 2013

Emojis, Marty Allen, Dog'N'Bone Books, New York, 2015

The Story of Emoji, Gavin Lucas, Prestel Verlag, Munich, 2016

The Emoji Code, Vyvyan Evans, Picador, New York, 2017

LoCoS Visual Language for Global Communication, Yukio Ota, 2018

The Annex of Universal Languages, Edgar Walthert & Richard Niessen,
    The Palace of Typographic Masonry (poster), Netherlands, 2019

Debranding is the New Branding, Ben Schott, Bloomberg.com, 3/7/2021

I Heart Design, Steve Heller, Rockport, 2011

Joyful presentations

Better Presentations, Jonathan Schwabish, Columbia University Press, New York, 2017

Science

Give Me a Smile, Jonathan Kalb, The New Yorker, 1/12/2015

More to a Smile Than Lips and Teeth, Carl Zimmer, The New York Times, 1/25/2011

The Laughing Guru, Raffi Khatchadourian, The New Yorker, 8/30/2010

Ha!, Scott Weems, Basic Books, New York, 2014

For children:

Tree in the Trail, Holling Clancy Hollings, Houghton Mifflin, Boston, 1942

Seabird, Holling Clancy Hollings, Houghton Mifflin, Boston, 1948

Minn of the Mississippi, Holling Clancy Hollings, Houghton Mifflin, Boston, 1951

Pinhole, Nigel Holmes, Jorge Pinto Books, 2010

Art Blob, Nigel Holmes and Erin McKenna, AB Publish, 2020

Information Graphics; Understand the facts in the blink of an eye, by Simon Rogers, Big Picture Press.
    Series illustrators: Peter Grundy, *Human Body,* 2014; Nicholas Blechman, *Animal Kingdom,* 2014;
    Jennifer Daniel, *Space,* 2015; Studio Muti, *Technology,* 2017

My Life Beyond Leukemia, Hey Gee and Rae Burremo, Mayo Clinic Press, 2021
My Life Beyond Bullying, Hey Gee and Ralph M., Mayo Clinic Press, 2021
Animal Joy, Nuar Alsadir, Graywolf Press, Minneapolis, 2022

Chartoons

How to Look at Iconography, Ad Reinhardt, PM (newspaper), New York, 1946
Envisioning Information, Edward Tufte, Graphics Press, Cheshire, 1990
National Lampoon Magazine (Time Parody), January 1984

Appendix

Dreyer's English, Benjamin Dreyer, Random House, New York, 2019
Nine Nasty Words, John McWhorter, Avery, New York, 2021
Appendix, A History of, Dennis Duncan, Norton, New York, 2021
Book of Parts, Dennis Duncan and Adam Smyth, Oxford University Press, 2019

Thank you

This book would not have happened if Alberto Cairo hadn't asked me to think about it, and then introduced me to Elliott Morsia at CRC Press. Alberto was the best editor I could possibly have had, telling me to be myself, and making suggestions all through the process that he kept saying were just suggestions, but which were perfect. Thank you, Alberto.

Jenn Shore of Shore-Creative helped me with the production phase of Indesign; you wouldn't be reading this if she hadn't patiently waded through my files to make them fit for print. It was thankless grunt work for a great designer. You have my thanks, Jenn!

And thank you to all at CRC Press, including Randi Cohen, Production Editor Michele Dimont, and Copy Editor Samar Haddad for turning the book into a real thing.

Thank you to my art teachers, starting with Ian Fleming-Williams, whose newly constructed art building at Charterhouse was my refuge from sports and military hero-worship at the school, and who somehow got me an interview at the Royal College of Art (RCA), in London. The kind people at the RCA told me I had to go to a regional college of art first, then apply as a post-graduate.

I went to Hull College of Art, in Yorkshire, and met W.A. (Bill) Sillince, who taught illustration there. He was a famous *Punch* cartoonist who drew with a pencil on coarse-grained paper, giving them a softer look than the usual black and white line work of other cartoonists. He helped me put together a portfolio that ultimately got me accepted to the Royal College.

There, Paul Hogarth (yes, related to William), a great illustrator and visual reporter, took a bunch of us from the RCA on a sketching trip to Amsterdam, and sat and drew alongside us. While we dutifully tried to represent what was in front of us, Paul rearranged the view to make it even more iconically Dutch. He knew that what was left on the paper was more important than fidelity to the scene. Also at the RCA, Quentin Blake (now Sir Quentin), another *Punch* artist, taught us with a gentle charm, just like his drawings; and one more RCA teacher, Anthony Froshaug, a proponent of strictly gridded Swiss typography, who knew where I had gone to school (he went to the same one), and who told me that I should do better in his classes because of that experience. It was a good school, but right then I was just happy to be at art college, away from expectations of a career in law or politics, or business. Froshaug's comments, while harsh at the time, pushed me. A good teacher!

To Brian Haynes, who told me I wasn't a very good illustrator when I interned with him at the *Sunday Times Magazine,* while I was a student at the RCA. Brian told me to combine what little illustration talent I may have had with information. When he left the *Times* and became Art Director of other magazines in London, he gave me lots of freelance graphics jobs.

To David Driver, who beautifully redesigned the stuffy *Radio Times* for the BBC, and commissioned me almost weekly for the magazine. He got me to interview the sports and science radio and TV commentators whose on-air broadcasts I was going to illustrate. I took those graphics to New York when I met Walter Bernard at *Time*.

To Walter himself, an unfailingly kind man and terrific Art Director, who championed my work at *Time* in the face of opposition from editors who were resistant to change at first. Walter's personal open-door office policy welcomed collaboration from anyone with a good idea.
To my core team at *Time*, the researchers Noel McCoy and Deborah Wells, and my assistant Nino Telak. I have come to realize that these three names should have been printed next to mine on every chart published in *Time*.

Many Art Directors helped launch my return to freelance life after *Time*. I thank them all, but would like to mention these by name: Richard Aloisio of *The New York Times,* Holly Holliday of *Attaché* magazine, Bambi Nicklen of *Stanford* magazine*,* Jen Christensen of *Scientific American* magazine; and Rudy Hoglund, Tom Bentkowski, Robert Priest, and Bob Ciano who between them oversaw art and graphics at many of America's best magazines.

To Amanda Hostalka who created an exhibition of my work at Stevenson University, and Michael Stoll who later mounted a traveling exhibition that opened in Munich and went on to Zeist, in Holland, and Ohio University. What they did by searching through my archives was a tremendous help for me finding (and remembering) stuff you see here.

To my fellow English-turned-American infographic colleague and friend, John Grimwade, for years of laughter and rants about the state of infographics, often over lunch at the bottom of the Empire State Building in New York. John read a draft of the book and made thoughtful suggestions for changes. To Christoph Blumrich, who held a position at *Newsweek* similar to mine at *Time*, and who once saw a freelance job I had done that wasn't very good, and told me that I should treat every single job with as much integrity as I could, however small. To Jon Schwabish, R.J. Andrews, and Jason Forrest, fellow writer-infographic practitioners, whose books and relentless search for historical infographics forerunners are continually inspiring.

To Richard Saul Wurman, who invited me to speak at his second TED Conference, in 1990, and subsequently asked me to work with him on four health-related books, then other clients, and finally as a co-author on *Mortality*. To Rick Smolan, whose used my graphics to explain non-photographic things in his wonderful photo-based books. To Julius Wiedemann, who included me in Taschen's door-stoppingly huge books of graphics (together with Sandra Rendgen), and shepherded my *Crazy Competitions* through a difficult birth at Taschen. To Ben Handicott and Robin Barton of Lonely Planet, who let me make travel books that weren't really about travel.

To Della van Heyst, Holly Brady, and Tina Weiner, who allowed me—encouraged, even—to experiment with 'performance' graphics on stage during the wonderful Publishing Conferences they ran at Stanford and Yale. To Guy Bailey, the most patient audio-visual technician ever, who helped me mount some weird presentations at Stanford (one was a pre-PowerPoint show that involved three 35-mm slide projectors pointing at different parts of the stage), and who never questioned what on earth I was doing, but made it all work.

To Frank Dobyns for reading my attempt to explain how we smile. At 89, and suffering from ALS, Frank overcame his disability to type, and managed to send me a carefully worded critique. Thank you Frank; rest in peace.

To Dr James Wong whose careful cataract surgery gave me new eyes, and to Dr Noelbis Cid, who looks after them, even though she hates my round, blue glasses.

To my son Rowland for making my graphics move in beautiful animation on the web, and for long-distance computer-problem-solving FaceTime sessions between Westport and Lido di Camaiore, Italy, during which he shows impressive patience in the face of my digital incompetence, and then always solves the problems. Rowland made the website for this book: www.joyfulinfographics.com.

Finally, thank you to my best friend. You know that without you, Erin, I could not have done any of this.

Credits

All images were drawn, photographed, or owned by me, except for those noted here.

I contacted the rightsholders that I was able to identify, but some didn't reply to my requests for permission, and some images could not be tracked down.

If anyone owns the rights to anything that I have reproduced, please forgive me, and contact me here at nigel@nigelholmes.com, so that I can address the situation.

Page 11, Etching, and drawing of canoe yawl by George Holmes
12, Drawing of Humber sailing trawler by George Holmes
13, Map of the River Hull by George Holmes
16, Map of Yorkshire and Lancashire by H. Alnwick
17, Edward Lear book cover by Barnett Freedman
17, Detail of an advertisement from *Punch* magazine, January 4, 1950
41, Trafalgar stamp by Peter Grundy
41, Postcard of *Queen Mary,* Mayfair Cards of London
53, Sketch and map by R.M. Chapin Jr., *Time* magazine
57, Map by R.M. Chapin Jr., *Time* magazine
73–76, Graphics by myself and Peter Brookes, *Radio Times*
77, Photo by Tony Evans, *Radio Times*
78, 79, Graphic by myself and Robin Jacques, *Radio Times*
    (used with permission from John Paul Jacques)
84, *Wee People* by Alberto Cairo and Scott Klein. © 2018 ProPublica and Alberto Cairo
    Freely downloadable: https://github.com/propublica/weepeople
85, *Little Man* by Warren Goodrich, *San Francisco Chronicle*
97, Spratts logo by Max Field-Bush (1936)
99, Olympic icons: Katsumie Masuru & Yoshiro Yamashita (top); Otl Aicher (middle);
    Masaaki Hiromura (bottom)
100,101, Olympic icons by Álvaro Valiño for *The Washington Post*
102, Olympic icons by Sarah Rosenbaum
103, Group of 10 figures (bottom of page) by Gerd Arntz,
    © 2022 Artists Rights Society (ARS), New York, c/o Pictoright Amsterdam
104, 2 figures (middle of page) by Gerd Arntz,
    © 2022 Artists Rights Society (ARS), New York, c/o Pictoright Amsterdam
105, Icons by Shigetaka Kurita; Digital image © The Museum of Modern Art/
    Licensed by SCALA/Art Resource, NY
107, Xu, Bing, *Book from the Ground: Windows OLE Object,* pages 64-65,
    © 2014 Xu Bing, by permission of The MIT Press
108, *Semantography* by Charles Bliss

108, *LoCoS* by Yukio Ota

109, Photo of smiley face in trees by Dave Killen, *The Oregonian*

109, Smiley logo by The Cherry Hut

111, I [Heart] NY by Milton Glaser (1975)

112, Icons for Schiphol Airport, courtesy of Mijksenaar, bv, Amsterdam

112, Symbols for Schiphol parking areas by Rob (Opland) Wout,
   © 2022 Artists Rights Society (ARS), New York, c/o Pictoright Amsterdam

112, Photo of fly in urinal, courtesy of Mijksenaar, bv, Amsterdam

113, Damascus street signage by Luigi Farrauto

113, Cover of *Kanji Pictographix* by Michael Rowley

114, 115, Icons by Álvaro Valiño for Rundfunk-Sinfonieorchester Berlin

145, Cover of *I am a book. I am a portal to the universe* by Stefanie Posavec and Miriam Quick

174, Chart by Philip A. Scheuer for *National Lampoon*

177, Chart by Jason Forrest, Gabrielle Merite, and Gergo Varga for McKinsey & Company

191, Clothing label (front and back) by L.L. Bean

JOYFUL INFOGRAPHICS

In *Joyful Infographics: A Friendly, Human Approach to Data,* one of the leading graphic designers of recent times shows how a judicious use of humor can make infographics more understandable. Written in non-academic, easy-to-understand language, and with historical and contemporary visual examples presented throughout, this small book provides a short history of light-hearted graphics. The text outlines nine clear ways to make graphics more understandable, explores the importance of the audience, shows you how to make information come alive during presentations through live-action 'performance' graphics, discusses why joy and smiling are good for you, and shows you how not to overdo it.

Even if a subject is delicate, controversial, or taboo, being graphically friendly to the audience is the right way to explain it. It is the opposite of being clinically cold and just presenting the facts. If you can get readers to smile—the smile of recognition when they understand the graphic—you are more than halfway toward getting them to continue reading, and understanding, the intention of the piece. *Joyful Infographics* teaches you how to do just that.

Nigel Holmes has written ten books (now eleven!) on information design and infographics. He is the former graphics director of *Time* magazine, has lectured globally, and has taught at Stanford and Yale. His diverse list of clients includes the BBC, Ford, Heinz, BMW, Sony, Estée Lauder, and Apple, and his work has appeared in a wide range of media including the *New York Times, Rolling Stone, Esquire, Sports Illustrated, New Scientist, National Geographic, Scientific American,* and the *New Yorker.* He has given three TED talks, his work has been exhibited internationally, and he is the recipient of multiple awards, including the Lifetime Achievement Award from The Society of News Design, and the Ladislav Sutner Award.